9 Steps Toward Healing

Moving Forward through Trauma from Loss of Loved One

By Chelsea Berrie

"I will not say: do not weep; for not all tears are evil".

J.R.R. Tolkien

Table of Contents

by Chelsea Berrie

by Chelsea Berrie

YOUR FREE GIFT

A High-Quality Colouring Book for Adults / Family!

Relax and relieve your stress with handpicked mandalas, wildlife animals, pets to colour with your family members or simply on yourself. Unleash your personalized creativity, imagination, and your inner artist with inspiring natural peace of mind, amazing illustrations that you can't find elsewhere. A book valued at 20$ now is yours for free, limited copies available.

Grab your free book here:
https://leadinggene.com/books/

Or you can scan the QR code here:

by Chelsea Berrie

Introduction

You are here because you have lost someone. A brother, sister, son, daughter, friend, partner. Someone who you cared about, someone who you still care about.

And I am not going to start by trying to guess how you are feeling, or by telling you how you are supposed to feel or how you are supposed to act, because it is different for everyone, and there is no right answer.

A few years back two of my closest friends both lost their fathers in the same week.

- Friend A, let us call him George, was continually active. He helped organize the funeral and the wake, made sure everyone got the message, posted on social media, and even started a fundraiser to raise money for a charity in honour of his dad.

- Friend B, let us call her Jess, was the opposite. She disappeared into her room and barely came out for 3 days. No social media, no phone calls, no contact.

Two people, who in theory were going through the same life change at the same time, were having completely different experiences, and hugely different responses.

Neither way was 'right' or 'wrong,' they were simply different ways of coping.

- For George, being active gave him purpose, he felt useful, and he could focus on doing his tasks.

- For Jess, having time alone was a way to collect her thoughts and stabilize.

My point is, when it comes to recovery, we are all different.

Which raises the question…

If our experiences are so different, how can a single book seek to help everyone?

More in Common than Meets the Eye.

To answer the question, I want to put forward the idea that experiences can be both unique and common at the same time.

If 1000 people run a marathon, they will all run it with different bodies, in different clothes and shoes, and with different levels of support, and so they will finish the race with different timeframes.

And yet every single person has still run 26 miles. Every single person has still felt the fatigue, the exhaustion, the dehydration. They might have experienced them at different times and in different amounts. But they HAVE experienced them.

Make sense?

by Chelsea Berrie

So, going back to Jess and George, yes, their experience have been unique, they have had different suppor networks and different personal psychologies.

But at the same time their experiences have been common. They've both had to experience grief, loss sadness, emptiness, anger. They might have experienced them in different amounts and at different times, but they HAVE experienced them.

Experiences of Loss –

3 Commonalities

Based on the collective experience of others, does any of this sound true for you?

1) You are struggling to accept the loss of the person(s) you care about?

Sometimes it feels like they are still there, or you find yourself talking about them or even to them as if they are not gone?

2) You have seen your loved one come back to you in a dream?

And it felt especially real, vivid, or lifelike?

3) You are having a hard time recovering emotionally?

You might be back working or generally seem like you are carrying on with your life, but it feels more like surviving than thriving. Almost like you are watching yourself in third person. You are there, but you are not truly present, and you feel a kind of quiet dullness?

If any of those ring true for you, then I think you will find this book helpful.

I Have Three Aims for You by The Time You are Done Reading…

by Chelsea Berrie

First, that you can learn some useful techniques to help you accept your loss.

Second, that you will be able to learn and apply specific methods to progress your recovery.

And third, that you should feel able to embrace life again, moving forward while still acknowledging the love and respect you have for the one(s) you lost.

To Achieve Those Aims, We Are Going to Be Covering...

1.   **Grief (Re)Education.** Looking at some of the major myths surrounding loss, and providing you with a healthier, more inclusive framework for recovery.

2.   **Building Your Support Team.** Exploring the benefits of therapy, some common misconceptions, as well as how to educate your friends and family so that you can empower them to support you in the ways you deserve.

3.   **Creative Coping.** Examining how painting, writing poetry, and other creative arts can offer invaluable and unexpected pathways to recovery.

4.   **Exercise to Heal.** Looking at the benefits of exercise while recovering from loss, as well as practical suggestions and guidance for implementing it into your life.

5.   **Mindfulness and Meditation.** Including key benefits like combating stress and reducing the impact of emotional triggers, plus specific ways to bring meditation and mindfulness practices into your day-to-day life.

6. **Music and Recovery.** How something that I avoided for so long can play a key role in relaxation, self-discovery, and grief processing.

7. **Daily Wisdoms and Contemplations.** Looking at various quotes on life, love, death and meaning to facilitate manageable doses of deep inner work.

8. **Learning to Celebrate, Honour and Remember.** Specifically, the three key activities you can use to move you towards celebrating your loved one, as well as how to create unique, personal ways to honour them.

9. **Hopes, Dreams and Future Plans.** Where we will talk about overcoming guilt and moving forwards, as well as examining the myths surrounding grief and growth, before concluding with three useful pieces of advice for making plans without putting too much pressure on yourself.

Who Am I to Offer Advice?

When I talk to people who have experienced loss, one of the most frequent complaints I hear is that people often offer unsolicited advice or opinions.

Or worse yet, meaningless platitudes like *"they are in a better place now," "at least they lived a long life,"* or *"there is a reason for everything."*

As the author of the book, I know this not only because I have experienced loss myself, but because I have taken the time to speak with, and truly listen to, hundreds of others that have dealt with major losses.

by Chelsea Berrie

- I have listened to what hurts.

- I have listened to what helps.

- And over time, I have started to get a sense of what recovering from a loss looks like.

To improve my understanding, I have also spent a lot of time writing and researching about grief, loss, and relationships. In fact, I have realistically spent the past seven years specializing in the topic.

It does not mean my knowledge is perfect.

And it does not mean you are going to agree with or utilize methods I say.

But what it *does* mean is that I can offer a selection of advice, tools, and techniques to help you process and recover from your loss; to help you start imagining a future you are excited about.

Going Forwards

As we progress through the book, I want you to keep in mind that what I am presenting are ideas. They are derived from research, from study and from the collective experience of others, and they could be incredibly useful to you.

But they are just suggestions.

You do not have to use any of them, and there is no 'right' or 'wrong' way to recover from your loss. Instead, take what you read as a collection of tools for your toolbox, and use what works for you at that given moment.

I will wrap this section up with a short paragraph from Haruki Murakami's Kafka on the Shore, which reads…

"And once the storm is over you will not remember how you made it through, how you managed to survive. You will not even be sure, in fact, whether the storm is over. But one thing is certain. When you come out of the storm you will not be the same person who walked in."

by Chelsea Berrie

Chapter 1: Grief (Re)Education

I think the first and most important step is for us to start with a little bit of re-education around the topic of grief.

Because confusing enough, there is a lot of problematic information out there, and if you are someone like me seven years ago, then it can end up doing you far more harm than good.

In this chapter we are going to be challenging some of the biggest myths about grief, about loss and about recovery, so that you can stop feeling shame, guilt and pressure based on uninformed and misguided opinions.

Myth Number 1: You Need to Be 'Strong'

I cannot tell you how many times I hear this sentence in tv shows, films and radio shows. The idea that for some unknown reason you have to be stoic, composed and unemotional in the face of loss.

It just does not make sense.

You are allowed to feel sad, you are allowed to feel angry, you are allowed to feel scared, or lonely or any other one of a dozen possible emotions, and there is no honour in bottled those feelings up and pretending they do not exist.

Worse still, you are often told that you need to *be strong for your kids,*" as if showing human emotion was somehow a bad weakness.

Reality check, if you have kids then they are suffering a loss too, and one of the best, healthiest things you can do to help them recover is to show them that it is okay not to be okay in this time of event, to show them that they can talk about and express how they feel. (Goldman 2014)

Myth Number 2: If You Do Not Cry There Is Something Wrong with You

Everyone deals with loss differently, and it is not always the most consistent with how you might normally act.

You might be someone who cries at every soppy movie. Even the thought of Bambi's mother might have you in floods of tears. But then someone close to you dies and you cannot shed a tear. Even if you want to, it just will not happen.

It is completely normal.

Grief can leave you feeling numbing, and just because you are struggling to process does not mean that there is something wrong with you. Your body and your mind are just dealing with your loss in their own timing.

What is more, there is also one kind of emotion called 'anticipatory grief,' a process in which you begin dealing with your emotional response to a personal loss before it has happened. This is especially common in cases of long or extended terminal illnesses. So, the reason you are coping better now might be because you have been slowly processing the impending reality of this loss for months.

In short, not crying after a loss is just one of many completely normal responses, and you certainly should not be feeling any guilt about it.

Myth Number 3: Ignoring Your Pain Will Make It Go Away Faster

I can promise you right now that ignoring your pain is not the answer.

If you had a broken leg, would ignoring make it heal faster?
How about a cut on your arm, would you feel better if you ignored it?
Of course, you would not. And yet because the pain of loss is internal rather than external, we try to kid ourselves into believing that we can just ignore it and it will go away.

The reality is that loss is real, and it has very real, physical impacts on your brain and your body that you cannot just ignore. Research (O'Conner 2019) has conclusively shown that following a loss you have...

- Increased risk of heart and cardiovascular problems
- Increased resting heartbeat rate.
- Increased cortisol (stress hormone) levels
- Increased inflammation
- Increased blood pressure

- Reduced immune system function.

So, you need to show yourself some compassion and make allowances. Trying to ignore your pain and expecting yourself to be at 100% just is not realistic.

Now, to be clear enough…

This IS NOT me saying that you cannot distract yourself. Sometimes you need distractions and escapes, and there is absolutely nothing wrong with that.

What I AM saying is that even if it is in little doses at a time, you must address your pain, address your loss, and allow yourself to feel.

Myth Number 4: Grieving Should Last for a Specific Amount of Time

Some of the most common online search terms relating to loss are those like *"how long should I grieve for?"* and *"how long is it normal to grieve?"*

And the reality is that there is no single correct answer. Grieving is a very personal process and the amount of time you will need is completely up to you.

Grieving for longer does not make you more loyal or mean that you are closer to the person you lost than someone else.

And similarly, grieving for less time does not mean that you care any less about the person you lost than someone else.

by Chelsea Berrie

Myth Number 5: You Have to Forget About Your Loss in Order to Move On

One of my biggest fears during my own recovery process was that if I stopped grieving and started to move on with my life, that I would be forgetting or even betraying the person I'd lost. I cannot tell you how guilty I felt when I went out and enjoyed myself when I met up with friends and laughed and had fun.

It took me a long time to realise just how hard I was being on myself, and just how wrong that train of thought was.

Because when I really stopped to think about it I wasn't ever going to simply 'forget' about the person I'd lost. My memories of them were not suddenly going to fade, they would be with me forever. And the funny thing is if they were still around, I know for a fact they would have been telling me to go out, see my friends and enjoy my life again.

Myth Number 6: Grief can be 'Completed' and There Are Certain Steps to Do It.

There is a popular book out there called the 'grief recovery handbook,' you might have heard of it or perhaps even own a copy. Some people absolutely love the book, while others really do not seem to get along with it.

From what I can see, the issue stems from the book being so systematic and rigid in its approach. In essence, it says that if you follow these exact steps, and do these exact worksheets, then you will 'complete' your recovery process.

That's not how grief works.

Do not get me wrong I can see why the idea is appealing. I would absolutely love for there to be an exact step by step system that neatly ties up a huge range of complex emotions into a simple package.

But there is not.

Humans are complex. Emotions are complex. And there is no 'one-size-fits-all' approach when it comes to dealing with loss.

Towards a More Helpful View of Grief

So now that we have covered six of the main ways NOT to view grief, I think it would be a good idea for us to work towards a more helpful viewpoint.

And the best way I can describe it is as this…

Grief is like an ocean.

And I know it sounds weird but hear me out…

At first, it feels like you have been abandoned at sea, you are drowning. You are completely overwhelmed by various emotions, and for the most part all you are aiming to do is survive.

Sooner or later, you learn how to tread water. You are not thriving, far from it. But you can look around you, get your bearings and think about something other than just surviving.

Over time, you build yourself a boat. Not a particularly fancy one, it is sort of leaky, and the oars are flimsy, but you can start moving towards dry land.

And your way to dry land is not always going to be smooth. Sometimes there will be these waves of grief that hit you and make you feel like you are right back to where you started. But you will get through them because you know you have already done so in the past.

Then eventually, in the future, you will be on dry land. You will be living your life, visiting friends and family, working, doing things you enjoy. It does not mean that the ocean has disappeared, or that you have forgotten it. Instead, the ocean has become a place that you can go to visit occasionally. You can stand on the beach, investigate the distance, and remember.

What I mean by all of this is that grief does not disappear. It is not something that you can complete or finish, and you will never truly be 100% 'over' the loss of someone close to you, nor should you expect to be.

That person will always be a part of your life because they've helped to define and shape you.

The main difference is that over time you will be able to think of them and laugh more than you cry. You will be able to look back and appreciate them, while living your own life to the fullest.

4 Golden Guidelines

Building on our new way of looking at grief, there are certain principles and guidelines that you can use to help you process your loss. In this section, we are going to cover those.

1) Share how you feel

There are huge benefits to being open about how you are feeling with those around you. Mainly because by clearly communicating how you are feeling, the people around you will have a better understanding, and will be better able to provide you with the support you need.

We will cover the importance of building your support team in chapter 2, but for now, just know that sharing how you feel is a healthy step.

2) Accept that pain is unavoidable

In Buddhist philosophy, suffering is seen as an essential, inevitable part of life, and while I am not Buddhist, I am inclined to agree with this idea.

By trying to avoid pain we often only end up making the pain worse, largely because we become so scared of it, or in psychological terms, so 'avoidant' of it, that even the idea of pain or suffering becomes overwhelming.

Instead, by accepting pain as an inevitable part of the grieving process, you allow yourself permission to feel it and to do so in small, manageable doses.

3) Look for healthy distractions

I know first-hand that the desire to look for escapes and distractions from your grief is huge, and for the most part this is completely fine. After all, if we just sat with our grief all day, we would end up feeling terrible 24/7.

However, we want to make sure that we are distracting ourselves in healthy ways with things like art, books, films, music, and exercise, rather than with unhealthy escapes like drugs and drink. We will be covering the benefits of these healthy distractions later in the book, as well as some ways to integrate them, but for now, just know that distractions are okay, so long as they are not harming you.

4) Give Yourself Time and Compassion

Finally, you need to give yourself time to heal, and accept the fact that you might not be operating at 100% for a while.

I know people who have suffered a major loss and then put themselves under pressure to get 'back to normal' as soon as possible; looking after their kids, going to social events, supporting family members and working high pressure jobs, and then being surprised when they have what can only be described as a complete crash a few weeks later.

Recovery from a loss takes time, so show yourself some compassion, stop holding yourself to such a high standard, and allow yourself to actually recover.

As the saying goes, "It is okay not to be okay," and sometimes 'success' is simply doing the essentials required to look after yourself and your dependents.

Action Steps

Throughout the book, we are going to be finishing each chapter with a set of actionable steps that you can put in place to help you towards your road to recovery. You do not have to follow all the steps if you do not want to, these are simply streamlined suggestions to bring together everything we have talked about in the chapter.

1) Be aware of and challenge the common myths surrounding grief, for example, the myths that "you need to be strong" and that "ignoring you pain will make it go away faster"

2) Focus on a more helpful view of grief, specifically the 'ocean' metaphor.

3) Follow the 4 'golden guidelines,' sharing how you feel, and giving yourself both time and compassion.

Chapter 2: Build Your Support Team (Therapists, Friends and Family)

"Do not be afraid to ask questions. Do not be afraid to ask for help when you need it. I do that every day. Asking for help is not a sign of weakness, it is a sign of strength. It shows you have the courage to admit when you do not know something, and to learn something new."

Barack Obama

In this chapter we are going to be talking about what is arguably the most important factor in recovering from loss: accessing support from therapists, friends, and family. We will start by looking at the benefits of therapy, as well as addressing some of the common misconceptions and stigma that surrounds it. After that, we will look at how you can educate your own family and friends to better support you, before concluding the chapter with a look at the value of support groups, online forums, and other places that you can interact with other key supporters.

The Benefits of Therapy

Since a lot of people only tend to think of therapy as sitting and talking about their loss, it is commonly dismissed as not being particularly useful. (We will be addressing why this is a misconception in the next section) The reality, however, is that therapy has a long list of significant benefits, all backed up by years and years' worth of study, research, and successful patient experience.

Here are eight of the biggest benefits of therapy…

1) Tackle difficult emotions in manageable chunks.

One of the best aspects about therapy sessions is that they provide a space in which you can tackle difficult emotions for a limited period. You are essentially providing yourself with a designated 50 minute slot in which you can process a small section of your grief, and then put it to the back of your mind for a while until you are ready to start processing again.

Therapists are also really well trained to know when to push you on certain topics and when to pull back, so they are able to help you tackle difficult emotions without becoming overwhelmed by them.

2) Have someone who will listen without judgement.

Personally, I know that my emotional responses to loss did not always feel like something I could, or should, share with my family. For example, sometimes I was angry at the person who I had lost. I knew it did not make sense, and I knew that logically, rationally I should not have been mad at someone for dying. And yet I was, and I felt guilty for feeling that way.

by Chelsea Berrie

With a therapist, you have got someone who does not know you, who does not have any personal opinions about you or the person you have lost, and that means that you can be 100% honest with them. You do not have to worry about upsetting them or disappointing them. You do not have to worry about being judged.

Plus, there is a real comfort in knowing that therapists have heard what you are going to say before, dozens of times. You are not going to shock them or surprise them and they are not going to be stumbling over their words trying to respond to you.

3) Create Practical Coping Strategies

Modern therapy is very much geared towards creating practical coping strategies to help you deal with the issues you are facing. Over a few sessions you will work with your therapist to come up with ideas that you can implement in day-to-day life. The exact strategies will vary based on your own specific situation, but a couple of simple examples include…

If you find your thoughts becoming negative and cyclic, try breaking the cycle by going out for a walk or run.

If you find yourself struggling with emotions that you cannot seem to express, try painting, drawing, or writing.

Of course, these are only quite simple, generic examples, and yours will be tailored to you, but you will be able to test them out for a few weeks, see if they work for you, and chat about them with your therapist.

Plus, these are skills and strategies that you can use forever. Right now, they are helpful for recovering from your loss, but you will still be able to use those same skills and strategies to deal with various stressful and difficult situations.

4) Improve Your Communication and Emotional Awareness

A huge benefit of therapy is that it improves your ability to communicate, as well as your emotional awareness. You see, most people tend to avoid engaging with and expressing their emotions, or they let their emotions get the better of them and end up getting angry and frustrated. Let us paint a quick picture...

Sandra, is 40, she is married and has two kids, aged 9 and 13. She works part time, usually about 16 hours per week, but also takes care of the household and the children, dropping them off at school, cooking dinners, cleaning and tidying etc. Well as part of her job, she has had to cover someone else's work, and is now working closer to 24 hours per week, while still doing all the same household and childcare work. She has less and less time for herself, essentially no time to relax, and she is stressed. She becomes increasingly frustrated, never saying a word of complaint, until one day a comment from her husband about the dishes sends her over the edge. She shouts at him, the kids are crying, and the entire house is walking on eggshells for the next week, with none of the tensions resolved.

It is not a made-up story; you will see the similar scenarios around you or in your neighbourhood. It tends to be a QUITE common one now.

by Chelsea Berrie

Now, let us paint a different story, one where Sandra had
been to therapy in the past, and had developed better
emotional intelligence and communication...

First, she expresses ahead of time to her husband that
her extra hours at work may mean that he must take up
some additional household responsibilities. Her
husband, who we assume is not a complete ass, agrees.
Problem solved. Much easier right?

Or, just for the sake of argument, let us say that Sandra
does not communicate ahead of time, and finds herself
getting overwhelmed and stressed. She can identify that
she is becoming stressed, she knows that low self-care is
likely to affect her mood, and she communicates this to
her husband so that they can come up with some
solutions together. How much nicer is that?

The ability to identify how you are feeling and
compassionately communicate your needs to other people
solves about 95% of arguments before they have ever
begun. And that's exactly what therapy gives you the skills
to do.

5) Provide You with New Perspectives

Another benefit of therapy is that it can provide you with
new perspectives that you might never have considered
on your own.

You know how the world's smartest scientists often
gather for 'masterminds' and 'think tanks' to bounce ideas
from each other? Well therapy is sort of like a small,
personalised version of that gathering.

You might go to your therapist firm believing one thing to be 'true,' because that is how you see it. You ought to come out of the session with two or three different, equally valid ways of looking at the same situation.

Here is a little personal example…

I went into one therapy session determined that one of my best friends did not care about me because they had barely been in touch for the month after my loss. My therapist suggested to me that maybe my friend was just trying to give me space, and to message them. Then when I got home, I messaged my friend, and within the hour they had messaged back offering to come round for the afternoon. Turns out that my therapist was right, my friend had just been giving me space because I had said a few weeks ago that I was getting sick of having so many visitors (something I did not really mean!)

Without my therapist giving me a new perspective, I would have stayed angry at my friend, and I would not have been able to get support from them,

6) Physically Rewire Your Brain

As a society, we tend to use the phrase *"it is all in your head"* to dismiss people's mental health issues as somehow lesser because they are not physical. And yet, time and time again science has shown that just because something is in your head, does not mean it is any less physical. Your brain is a hugely important part of your body after all!

by Chelsea Berrie

In fact, there are numerous studies showing that psychotherapy-based interventions can have significant positive impacts on brain morphology and function (Buchheim et al. 2012, Beauregard M. 2014, Guide 2012). In other words, therapy physically changes the form, shape, and structure of your brain in positive ways!

7) Makes You More Productive

An excuse I used to make to myself for years was that I did not have the time for therapy. I was always too busy doing something else that I am sure seemed super important at the time.

Now, though, I know that my excuse was completely rubbish, because a benefit of therapy is that it makes you far more productive in the long term. Sean Achor, author of The Happiness Advantage, writes that *"happiness gives us a real chemical edge…How? Positive emotions flood our brains with dopamine and serotonin, chemicals that not only make us feel good, but dial up the learning centres of our brains to higher levels"*.

8) It Gives You the Skills to Teach the Next Generation a Better Way

Finally, a huge benefit of therapy is that it brings us the skills to show our children a better way forward. Repressed emotions, passive aggression and poor communication do not have to be commonplace. Arguments can be resolved peacefully, often before they even really begin, simply by listening, empathising, and using emotional intelligence.

We can give the next generation better mental health awareness, better support systems, and more opportunities to be the people they were meant to be. If this is not a reason for us to book a few therapy sessions, then I do not know what it is.

Therapy Misconceptions (What NOT to Expect)

I have found that when I talk to people about therapy who have never experienced it, there tend to be quite a lot of misconceptions about what it involves. Some of these misconceptions are quite funny, but others can create a false perception that can end up acting as a real obstacle for people who would really benefit from the support a therapist can provide. In this short section we will be looking at 5 of the biggest misconceptions about therapy.

1) You will Sit on a Fancy Sofa Chair (Chaise Longue)

In almost all popular media, therapists and counsellors seem to have their patients sit in a chaise longue. It might have been big back in the early 20th century when Sigmund Freud popularised it, but nowadays most therapists just tend to have a simple chair in which you can sit and have a conversation.

2) It is All About Your Mother/Father

While our parents and our upbringing are important in our development as a person, it is only a part of who we are,

and therapists will only really talk about your parents if it i
relevant, for example, if you have just lost a parent.

This is yet another idea linked back to Sigmund Freud
whose work was novel back in the early 20th century, bu
has now been largely discredited as overly simplistic
excessively focused on sex, and generally quite sexist.

3) Therapists Are There to Tell You What You Are Doing Wrong

Another prevalent misconception is the idea that
therapists are going to point out what you are doing
wrong and highlight all your mistakes. In my experience,
and in the experience of the people I know, this is NOT
the case.

In reality, today's therapists are far more focused on
listening to you, understanding you, and working with you
to come up with proactive strategies and approaches that
will help you move forward and feel better about yourself.

4) Once You Start Therapy You Never Stop

Therapy, if not covered by your insurance or government,
can be expensive, and a major concern is that it will last
forever, never reaching a resolution.

The good news is that therapy tends to work on a much
shorter-term basis, with nearly half of the people who
engage in therapy using between 3 and 10 sessions, and
only one in nine people using more than 20 sessions.
(Alpert 2012)

This is because today's therapists generally focus far less on what you did twenty years ago, and more on what you can do today and tomorrow to feel better.

5) Therapists Can Solve All of Your Problems

Sometimes people go into therapy with completely the wrong expectations, thinking that the therapist can magically 'fix' them, or that all of their problems will be dealt with within 1 or 2 sessions.

The reality is that…

a) therapy takes time, and you cannot expect resolutions to complex issues in a single 50-minute session.

b) your therapist is not a magician, they cannot just say a few words and suddenly all your problems disappear.

A much better framework to go in with is that your therapist is an experienced teammate who you work collaboratively with to come up with various ideas, activities, and approaches that you can use to tackle your problems.

What Does a Typical Therapy Session Actually Look Like?

The exact structure and content of a therapy session can vary depending on the therapeutic approach being taken.

by Chelsea Berrie

However, there are certain commonalities that you can expect.

Your therapist will introduce themselves and will give you plenty of opportunity to explain how you are feeling, and what you are struggling with. They might also ask a few questions to gain further insight.

You will then tend to have some type of conversation with your therapist, but only at a pace that you are comfortable with. Therapists are trained to know when to push and when to pull back, so that you get to deal with difficult topics in small, manageable doses.

At the end of your session, your therapist might quickly review the main takeaways, maybe even providing you with some simple coping strategies and tips that you can implement in your day-to-day life. They will also book you in for your next appointment, usually in a week or two.

Therapy Stigma: Why Do Some People Dislike the Idea of Therapy?

Data from the UK (Lubian et al. 2016) shows that around 1 in 3 people aged 16–74 with symptoms of a common mental health issue receive mental health treatment. And while this figure is better than nothing, that still leaves two thirds of the population trying to deal with issues like anxiety, grief, and depression without any mental health treatment.

So why are so many people not receiving the help they need?

1) Misconceptions

One of the biggest reasons that stigma surrounds therapy is simply that a lot of people are still under the misconceptions that we discussed in the section above. Fundamentally, if people believe that a therapy studio is a place where they go to be judged, shouted at, or told off then why on earth would they ever want to go there?

2) 'Stiff Upper Lip'

Although this is improving with time, there is still very much a tradition in countries like the USA, UK, and Canada of having a 'stiff upper lip,' as in not letting your emotions show, and remaining composed even in the face of hardship and distress. At this point, research has shown conclusively that this is not the best approach, but it continues to impact popular perceptions of therapy being a sign of weakness.

Generally speaking, although therapy stigma based around 'stiff upper lip' affects both men and women, it tends to be men who most suffer from the social expectations of remaining stoic and emotionless, which goes a long way towards explaining the higher rates of suicide among men.

3) Education and Community barriers

Therapy costs money, and therapists are university educated people who are generally well-paid. This creates an immediate mismatch between therapists and people from backgrounds that earn less money and do not tend to go to university.

by Chelsea Berrie

Unfortunately, this means that access to, and uptake of, therapy is significantly less in communities with less money and less education. This means that millions of people miss out on the crucial benefits that therapy can provide, not just in dealing with loss and grief, but in dealing with every single mental health issue.

Over the long term, you could also argue that this disparity only adds to and reinforces social barriers, widening the wealth and education gap, but that's probably a whole other discussion for a whole different book!

What matters is that you do not let your community and background define your decisions relating to useful healthcare services. If you think that accessing therapy will benefit you in coping with your loss, then make every effort possible to do so.

Complicated or Traumatic Grief and EMDR

Throughout this book I have really tried to reinforce the message that different people respond to grief in different ways, and that there is no 'right' or 'wrong' way to process the emotions that come with it.

With that said, I do need to point out that grief should start to feel less over time, and as your ability to cope improves, you should be able to re-engage with the activities in your life that bring you joy.

If this does not appear to be the case, and you find

yourself continually struggling with intense feelings of grief for a prolonged period of time that are interrupting your daily life, then you may be suffering from what's known as 'complicated' or traumatic grief.

This tends to be more common in cases where the death of a loved one was sudden, unexpected, or especially traumatic in nature.

If this sounds like you, then I highly recommend you look into a process known as EMDR, or Eye Movement Desensitization Reprocessing. I know that sounds like a complete mouthful, but the basic idea is that using left to right distractions such as movements, sounds or taps, can help to partially distract your brain, allowing it to better process traumatic events without experiencing the same intense level of emotional reaction.

Over time, by repeating this type of session, your ability to think about and process difficult or traumatic memories will improve, and your emotional reaction will lessen to a point at which it is far more manageable. This is known as 'phased desensitization,' and it has a lot in common with processes used for overcoming serious phobias, as well as processes used with physiotherapy for overcoming serious physical injuries.

You can find more information about EMDR here.

Ways to Find a Therapist

Accessing therapy varies per country and by region, but a good starting point is usually to speak to your general practitioner and see if a referral is possible.

by Chelsea Berrie

Within the UK, this will be completely free of charge, whereas within the US this will depend on your insurance coverage. You might have to pay some upfront costs and be reimbursed later, or you may be able to access free clinics.

In the US there is also the National Alliance for Mental Health, which has phone lines open 10am till 8pm Monday to Friday and will be able to point you in the right direction.

There are also directories in places like Psychology Today and GoodTherapy.org where you can find therapist contact details, including therapists who work on a sliding cost scale based on your income.
If you are looking for a more flexible, and often cheaper option, therapists are also available through video calls and messenger services online. Some good apps to look at for this include Talkspace and Betterhelp.

And if none of these options seem to be working for you, you can always go to google and type in *"find a therapist plus the name of your country and area,"* for example, *"find a therapist Toronto Canada"* and you should get some quick results to explore.

How to Educate Friends and Family So That They Can Support You Better

Let us be honest, it is not easy knowing what to say or how to act around someone who is going through a major loss. Even having been through a loss myself, and having studied and written about loss for years, I still sometimes find myself struggling with others.

Your friends and family are just the same. They want to help, they really do, but they genuinely do not know what to say or how to act, so they end up saying some goofy, dumb, or even hurtful things without meaning to.
Any of these sounds familiar?

The Overly Religious Friend

"They are in a better place now".
"It is all part of God's plan".
"They are such a good person God wanted them to be with him".

They might think that their beliefs are helpful, but chances are they just come across as patronizing or out of touch, and that is if you are a fellow believer. If you do not follow the same religion, or you are atheist, then sentences like this probably just annoy you.

The Minimizer

"At least they lived a long life".
"You can always… (remarry, have another child etc)"
"This is a part of life for everyone".

They think that they are helping you feel better by reducing the severity of the loss, but by minimizing how you are feeling they come across as insensitive, cold and unempathetic.

The One Thinking About Themselves

by Chelsea Berrie

"I do not think I could cope with that".
"Were they a smoker/drinker?"

They think they are helping you, when all they are doing i
over-identifying and imagining what they would be like i
that situation. Not exactly comforting.

It does not take many of these remarks for you to decide
that talking to other people about your loss is not helpful,
so you end up reducing contact with friends and family
because you cannot trust them to actually help you to
recover from your loss.

The problem is, by doing so you are cutting yourself off
from a whole range of potential support, which can end
up making recovery really difficult.

The solution, then, is to educate your friends and family on
how best to support you, and you can do this in two ways..

1) **Acknowledge the difficulty openly.**

Tell close friends and family that you know it is hard for
them to know what to say. At the same time, you can also
send them a few useful links as guidance…

'What to say to someone in grieving'

'What to say (and what not to say) to someone who's
grieving'

You can send the links by text, by Messenger, by
WhatsApp, by email, anything that works.

2) **If possible, tell people what you need from them.**

I know this is not always easy because you are not always sure what you need. If in doubt, just assign people simple jobs to make your life easier.

- Could you pick up some fresh groceries for me occasionally?
- Could you look after the kids a couple nights this week?

That sort of minor task.

Or, if all you want is some company and someone to be around you, ask for that.

Or, if you want someone to just shut up and give you a hug, ask for that.

At the end of the day, people are not mind readers, so by taking five to ten minutes to educate them on how to talk to you, and how they can help, you are setting them up for success and empowering them to become reliable, helpful parts of your support system.

I promise, it only takes a few minutes, but it will be one of the most useful few minutes you have ever spent.

Return to Work: How to Make Your Workplace Part of Your Support Team

by Chelsea Berrie

I am going to be 100% honest with you, it does not matter how much you try to separate your work life from your personal life, there is always going to be crossover especially during times of emotional upheaval.

I say this with experience, <u>talk to your employer about your loss as soon as possible.</u>

You might not want to, and it might be slightly awkward, but it is better to let them know what is going on now rather than when they drag you into the office for producing hilariously low amounts of incredibly poor-quality work.
The conversation does not have to be a fancy one; you just need to work out two issues…

1) Let your boss or immediate line manager know that you are dealing with a major loss, and that although you are going to do your absolute best, you realise that it may temporarily impact your ability to work.

2) Discuss what arrangements you can make with your workplace to make life easier for you during your recovery process. For example,

- In the UK, employees have a legal right to 2 weeks off work for bereavement. This does not legally have to be paid, but many employers choose to do so.

- Consider a staggered return to work, with duties and responsibilities gradually increasing over a few weeks as you settle back into a work routine.

- Counselling through the employer. Some employers offer subsidised access to counselling and therapy which you may be able to access.

It is also important to take some time to be honest with yourself about workplace expectations. If you are usually the highest performing member of your team it can be easy to feel like you need to continue filling that role, putting yourself under extra pressure for no good reason. Sometimes it is completely acceptable to be mediocre, or to just accomplish the bare minimum to keep your boss/clients/team happy.

Now, this is not an excuse to just drop your performance to the point where you are at risk of losing your job, because that would be a poor decision. All I am saying is that you can temporarily allow yourself to lower your expectations as you focus time and energy on recovering from your loss.

I promise you, if you have communicated with your line manager and you have decent colleagues, nobody is going to expect you to be working at 100%. If you can maintain a basic level of competence people will be okay with that. And if they are not, then chances are your workplace culture is toxic as hell, so perhaps finding somewhere new to work would not be a bad idea anyway!

by Chelsea Berrie

Why You Should Consider Support Groups and Forums

From experience, one of the biggest misconceptions I remember dealing with after my loss was the feeling that was alone, and that nobody else understood what I was going through. For me, a big part of my recovery was found in support groups, both in person and online. They put me in touch with other people going through similar experiences, who reminded me that I was not on my own. Some people had lost parents, others lost siblings, others lost children, and the opportunity to hear each other's stories was incredibly valuable. Typical meetings and conversation topics included…

- How to access therapy
- Healthy coping strategies
- Group rants about our actual feelings
- Sharing ideas for activities and distractions
- Stories of recovery from people who were further down the path

Even if you are someone who tends to take actions on your own, having the ability to drop in and out of an occasional group support session could be valuable for you in the end.

If you want some good places to start, the website verywellmind.com actually just put together a list of their top 7 online forums for grief support groups…

- **Best Overall:** Grieving.com
- **Best Live Chat:** Grief in Common
- **Best for Young People:** Hope Again
- **Best Social Media Group:** Grief Anonymous

- **Best for Specific Grief:** <u>Online Grief Support</u>
- **Best for Email Support:** <u>GriefNet</u>
- **Best Monitored Discussion Group:** <u>Grief Healing</u>

Action Steps

Just like in chapter 1, we are finishing this chapter with a set of actionable steps that you can put in place to help you towards your road to recovery. You do not have to follow all the steps if you do not want to, these are simply streamlined suggestions to bring together everything we have talked about in the chapter.

1) Be aware of and challenge the common misconceptions surrounding therapy, then aim to get yourself booked into an appointment as soon as possible.

2) Educate your family and friends and what you need them to do (or not do) so that they can better support you.

3) Talk to your boss / line manager and explain the situation. Aim to set expectations in line with what you truly feel you are capable of.

Chapter 3: Creative Coping - Using the Arts to Heal

"At the deepest level, the creative process and the healing process arise from a single source. When you are an artist, you are a healer; a wordless trust of the same mystery is the foundation of your work and its integrity."

Rachel Naomi Remen, MD

Depending on the type of person you are, that title either really intrigued you, or made you go *'urgh'* out loud, and you are reading this section mainly to laugh at it. To be honest with you, I used to be the latter. In fact, when heard about art-based therapy through a friend in one of my support groups I remember asking *"is not that just for kids."*

Well, turns out I was being a bit of an idiot. Alright, maybe not an idiot, but I was being close minded towards a potential way of recovering from loss. And the more learnt about art-based therapy and recovery methods, the more I discovered that it is one of the most well-established methods of therapy around, has a decent scientific backing (Stuckey and Nobel 2010) and is highly regarded among the psychotherapy community.

So, in this chapter we are going to be looking at how creative arts such as painting, sketching, colouring, writing, poetry and playing music can offer invaluable and unexpected pathways to recovery.

How Does Art-Based Therapy Work?

Fundamentally, the creative arts are expressive mediums, as in they allow people to express themselves.

Have you ever known a quiet person who turned out to be an amazing artist or writer?

Or had a friend who rarely spoke and then it turned out they were in a band and were awesome on the guitar?

Exactly.

Not everyone is a great verbal communicator, and even those that are sometimes have also a hard time to talk about emotionally difficult or troubling topics.

The creative arts provide a way for people to explore their emotions, express themselves and communicate, as well as build new coping skills.

One study even found that even the presence of art in hospitals improved mental health outcomes for patients. (Stine 2017)

The Benefits of Art-Based Therapy for Recovering from Loss

by Chelsea Berrie

One of the biggest reasons why people might be initially sceptical about the usefulness of art-therapy is because of how subjective and qualitative it is. With cures like pill or surgeries you can see really objectively and quantitatively that they have worked (the patient took the pill, now they are not sick, simple) But with intangible features like art-therapy and human emotions, the measurement is trickier.

Lucky for us, a fantastic team of researchers (Haeyen et al. 2015) conducted a series of in-depth interviews with 29 different adults, recording and typing up every single word of conversation and then analysing it in detail to look for recurring themes and patterns. What they found was that there were 5 key benefits of art-based therapy...

1) Perception and Self Perception - Focus on the Present Moment

One of the first major themes that came out of the study was that participants reported that engaging with art allowed them to focus on the present moment. Rather than thinking excessively about the past or the future, participants were able to concentrate on the task in front of them and draw attention to how they were personally feeling. This ability to identify your own emotional state, examine it and express it is crucial for recovery from loss.

2) Personal Integration - coherent self of self

One of the hardest things for any human to do is to bring together the different elements of their personality and beliefs into a coherent, meaningful whole. This is especially true for those experiencing loss, who will likely be going through a huge variety of conflicting emotions and processing a huge variety of ideas.

Participants found that art-based therapies gave them a way to express their multifaceted identity better than words, and in turn allowed them to create a more coherent self-image and sense of self.

3) Emotional Regulation

In chapter two we talked about how EMDR therapy works by sort of 'distracting' your brain, allowing you to process difficult events without the same level of emotional intensity. Art therapy uses a similar mechanism in that the act of drawing or painting distracts somewhat from the intensity of the emotion, while simultaneously providing a safe outlet or space for those emotions to be expressed.

This allows you to essentially play around with different events and ideas, putting them down on paper and seeing how you react to them, which over time can help you to better regulate your emotional responses to those events. For those of us dealing with loss, when emotions are so raw and we feel out of control, this can be incredibly helpful.

4) Behaviour change

Another interesting benefit that the study identified was that participants experienced positive behaviour change, both towards themselves and towards those around them. The researchers suggested that this may have been due to the self-directed nature of creative arts.

by Chelsea Berrie

Artists get to choose which pencil or paintbrush to use, which colour to use, where to put the colours etc. This sense of control and ability to alter outcomes could have increased self-efficacy (inner confidence that you are in control of your own actions and outcomes).

Personally, I also assume that it was because art is RELAXING. It takes some stress away, and I know for sure that I am a much nicer person when I am less stressed.

5) Personal Insight and Self-awareness

Last but certainly not least, the researchers identified that participants found themselves to have an increased sense of personal insight and self-awareness. By expressing their thoughts, feelings and emotions participants were able learn things about themselves. What is more, this process of self-learning was enhanced by looking at and reviewing the art they had created.

When dealing with loss, it can be hard to process what you are going through, and easily feel confused, uncertain, and unsure of yourself. By using art-based therapies, you will have the opportunity to process what you are feeling, learn more about yourself and gain some clarity in your life.

On top of these benefits, I really want to briefly talk about one of the biggest positives that I experienced by engaging with the creative arts...

An increased feeling of aliveness and participation in the world.

Which I know might sound silly, but right after my loss, I just felt detached from everything. I felt like I was going through day-to-day life, but not really living it and not truly engaging with the world around me.

Art gave some of that back to me.

The hour or two I spent each week either outdoors or by my window drawing, sketching, and writing made me feel like I was part of the world again, like I was engaging in human life.

Give it a try, just for a week, and I think you will see what I mean.

Types of Art-Based Therapy

One of the best aspects about art-based therapy is that there is no one-size-fits-all approach. There is a wide selection of arts and mediums that you can try out. Here are some examples that you might want to consider…

Sketching

Sometimes the simplest options are the best. Literally all you need is a piece of paper and a pen or pencil and you are good to go. You can take a practical approach, sketching things that you see in front of you, or you can just sketch something from imagination. You can also go a little more abstract, sketching the ideas, images and feelings that come into your mind in a free-association sort of way.

Painting/Colouring

Want to feel like an old-school artistic master? A modern day Van Gogh? Then painting might be for you. You will need a little bit of basic equipment, i.e., some paintbrushes and some paints, but you can get these at most stationary stores, or you can order a set online for little cost. Just like with sketching, you can take a more practical or a more abstract approach, it is totally up to you. Personally, I have found that there is something very soothing about the smooth, rhythmic motions used to paint.

Writing Poetry

Poetry is interesting. You see, unlike painting or sketching it still uses words, but those words do not have to be spoken out loud. What is more, those words do not really have to mean anything to anyone other than you. This gives a lot of creative freedom to express yourself and your ideas. If you like a bit of structure you can try a pre-set structure like a 5-line haiku or a 14-line sonnet, or you could just go for some simple rhyming couplets. On the other hand, if you are feeling a bit more abstract you can go for what is called *"stream of conscious,"* which is essentially a fast-flowing type of word association that you write down (Think James Joyce's Ulysses for example)

Writing Stories

Storytelling is one of the oldest and most loved forms of creative expression in the world. Who does not love a good story after all? Now, what is interesting about stories is that they have set narrative structures, which seems like it would limit expression, however, what people often find is that by working with, and working around, these structures, you can create some innovative ideas and concepts. Plus, for me, I found that being able to create characters and explore certain topics and emotions by proxy was incredibly helpful in my recovery. If writing a long story seems a bit daunting, then why not play around with short stories of just a few hundred words? Or, even quicker, flash fiction, in which you only have a few words to tell a whole story. For example, Ernest Hemingway's…

"For sale: baby shoes, never worn".

You can say a lot with very few words.

Crafting

If you are like me then the first idea comes to your mind is that infamous scene in ghost where they are crafting clay. Now, I love a good bit of pottery as much as the next person, and if you have got access to the equipment or a specific class then that is great, but for most of us we will need some slightly more accessible options. You can craft with paper, card, string, felt, thread, beads, feathers, acorns, egg cartons and a whole bunch of other everyday items. Or you can just pop to a craft store or look online for a simple starter kit. You are not necessarily aiming to create a masterpiece, it is much more about the present moment focus, and the process of creating what comes to mind.

by Chelsea Berrie

Practical Ways to Use Art-Based Therapy in Your Own Recovery

Alright, so we have discussed the benefits of arts-based therapy in your recovery process, as well as some of the types of creative art that you can try. In this section we will look at some simple, practical advice that you can use to implement art-based therapy for yourself.

1) Pick a Day and Time

It is all well and good waiting for inspiration to strike, but when you are dealing with grief inspiration does not tend to strike all that often. Instead, a better idea, at least at the start, is to pick a specific day and time to engage with art and to stick to it. So, you might start by saying that every Wednesday at 7pm you are going to spend 1 hour engaging with art.

2) Start with Zero Expectations

When starting any new activity or skill, it is best not to put pressure on yourself to perform or hit a certain standard. Instead, it makes much more sense to focus on having fun enjoying the process, and trying things out

To use an example, think of a 6-year-old playing soccer for the first time. Are you going to put them in a specific position, bark orders at them and expect them to run certain distances, make certain passes and score a certain number of goals? Of course not! (Well, I hope not anyway, because that would be BAD parenting and would probably just put the kid off soccer.) Instead, chances are that you would give them a ball and say, *"go play."* And guess what, by playing, trying things out and learning by doing, the kid's going to develop the skills naturally.

The exact same goes for starting off with any arts-based activity. There is no point expecting yourself to hit certain standards or do certain things. Your goal is simply to experiment, have fun, make loads of mistakes, and generally just enjoy the process.

3) Take Time to Reflect

Creating art is fantastic, but a huge part of the benefit from a loss recovery perspective also comes by taking the time to reflect on your work and analyse it. You will often end up finding that you have expressed feelings, emotions, or ideas that you did not even consciously intend to. This personal insight is a fantastic part of the artistic process, and it helped me myself to learn a lot about the memories of the past that were stored away in the back of my mind.

Action Steps

Once again, we are finishing this chapter with a set of actionable steps that you can put in place to help you towards your road to recovery, and just as before, do not feel like you have to follow all the steps if you do not want to, these are simply streamlined suggestions to bring together everything we have talked about in the chapter.

1) Keep an open mind towards the benefits of arts-based therapy, and look for a few types that you think will suit you.

2) Purchase or acquire any equipment you need

3) Practically, try to set a weekly day and time to practice along with time to reflect on your work.

******Please Leave a Review for my work so far******
As an independent author with a small marketing budget, reviews are my livelihood on this platform. If you enjoy this book so far, I would really appreciate it if you could leave your honest positive feedback. Thank you!
You can do so by clicking the link below. I love hearing from you, my readers and I personally read every single review.

******link to review page******

&&&&__You are welcome to join our group to learn some tips you may never heard of to enhance your mental performance__&&&

Chapter 4: Exercise to Heal

Speaking from experience, I know that possibly the LAST thing I felt like doing after my loss was to go and exercise. I just remember feeling so tired, so beaten up and so completely demotivated that the idea of having to use even more energy just to get tired and sweaty seemed crazy to me.

And yet looking back, I can also say with certainty that the time I DID spend exercising was incredibly useful for my recovery, and if you will hear me out, I will explain why.

The Benefits of Exercise When Recovering from a Loss

1) More Long-Term Energy

I know it sounds counterintuitive that exercise gives you more energy, but it really does. Yes, it requires energy in the short term, but over the long term it absolutely provides it.

It makes your lungs better at absorbing oxygen, it makes your heart better at pumping oxygen, and it makes your body better at delivering that oxygen to your muscles. In essence, the fitter and healthier you are, the less energy your body takes to do simple daily tasks.

2) Better Sleep

Linked to the above point about giving you extra energy, one of the main ways that exercise does this is by allowing you to have better sleep.

Before I started exercising I cannot even tell you how many nights I struggled to sleep, laying there with my mind just racing, or worse yet, just obsessively thinking about what I'd lost.

But after I started training I was pretty much out like a light as soon as my head touched the pillow.

And it is not just me that thinks so, research by the national sleep foundation found that regular exercise significantly improves sleep quantity and quality.

3) Reconnect with Your Body (Get Out of Your Head)

I cannot speak for everyone, but for me, spending so much time in my head thinking about love, life, loss, and the world in general made me feel really detached from my body. I did not feel physical, or confident, let alone anything approaching sexy.

Exercise was a way for me to regain those things by rebuilding my connection with my body. It gave me a real sense of control and of purpose, and it was a practical way for me to cut myself off when I was heading down the path of overthinking and existentialism.

4) See the Outside World

Again, I cannot really speak for everyone, but if you are someone like me who found themselves closing and shutting themselves off after a loss, then exercise could be a real positive recovery way for you.

Going to the gym, or out for a walk or run, made me leave the house, it forced me to be around other people. I might not have always chatted to anyone, but I would have had to see them, make eye contact, nod and maybe even smile occasionally.

In short, exercise got me outside, and around other people, which is hugely important for recovery.

Can Exercise Release Stored Stress and Trauma?

One of the prevailing theories about the benefits of exercise in the modern era is that it allows you to 'resolve' stress cycles, preventing stress from being 'stored' in the body.

The idea is that historically, when humans used to experience stress (i.e. faced with a tiger) their bodies would release cortisol, as well as adrenaline, and they would either attack it (fight) or run from it (flight) releasing that adrenaline and resolving the biological loop.

However, nowadays the stresses we encounter are different. Emails, house admin, workplace drama, stuck in traffic, that sort of daily work stress. So, it is not a kind of stress that we can fight or that we can run from, which means that the biological loop is never truly resolved. We experience the stress, but not the resolution.

by Chelsea Berrie

And what is loss if not a stress to your body? As we
mentioned earlier in chapter 1, experiencing a loss
increases your cortisol (stress hormone) levels, as well as
temporarily damaging a whole host of bodily functions. By
experiencing loss, your body has entered a huge biological
loop, and it is not one that you can resolve simply by
running away from it or by fighting it.

Exercise, in all its forms, offers a potential mechanism for
the release of some of this stored up stress. A possible
way of resolving at least some of the biological cycle that
your body is going through.

There are even specific Trauma Release Exercises (TRE)
being popularized by Dr. David Berceli, which you might
find useful. They have not been substantiated by research
yet, though, so I cannot vouch for their efficacy, but there
are numerous anecdotal reports of people finding them
helpful.

Practical Suggestions for Exercise After Loss

Alright, so we have looked at the various benefits, and I
have convinced you to give exercise a go as part of your
recovery process. But how do you go about it?

In this section we will be looking at general guidance and
expectations, specific types of individual and group
exercise that you can do, as well as answering some
common questions to help you get started and make the
most of it.

General Guidance and Expectations

First, I think it is important that you go into this with the right expectations. We are not starting exercise with the goal of massively improving our fitness. We are not aiming to run a marathon, or double our strength, or lose 3 stone in weight.

This is not the time to be putting yourself under pressure to perform.

Right now, your main goal of exercising is simple…

"Feel slightly better".

That is, it.

Nothing more, nothing less.

Now, do not get me wrong, if you regularly exercise each week for several weeks, you will VERY LIKELY find that you do in fact get much better at what you are doing. My point is that this should not be your goal.

What I do not expect is for you to set yourself some huge exercise goal and then end up feeling disappointed because you did not achieve it.

Remember, we are in a period of recovery, and the exercise we do is supposed to facilitate that. So, take it easy on yourself and do not go setting any huge targets.

This goes even more so if you were already a fitness enthusiast. If you were running 10k's in sub 50 minutes before your loss, do not go expecting yourself to be setting any personal bests right now. Just get out there and run for enjoyment.

Types of Individual Exercise

Now that we have got some of the general guidance and expectations out of the way, let us look at some of the individual exercise options available to you. There tend to be way more than you might originally think.

Walking: A great starter option, it is low impact, requires no special equipment, and gets you outside in the fresh air. If you can get out into nature, then even better.

Running: Another good option that requires minimal equipment, just a pair of running shoes. You can get outside, enjoy the fresh air, and improve your cardio.

Cycling: A great low impact cardio option that lets you cover more distance than walking or running. It does require more specialist equipment (the bike), but it does not need to be super expensive. If you are planning on road racing then sure you will need an expensive bike, but if you are just planning for a few shorter, leisurely rides around your area then you can easily find a bike for less than $200.

Swimming: A unique low impact cardio option that also provides a slight resistance training challenge at the same time. If you have previously struggled with sore knees, hips or back then this could be the perfect choice for you.

Resistance Training: This option is more like a broad category of options, such as bodyweight training, bodybuilding, strength training and even Olympic style weightlifting. Cost wise if you are training at home it can be free, or if you are joining a local gym you will have a membership cost. There are a bunch of benefits to be had from it., so keep an open mind and maybe give it a try.

Types of Group Exercise Classes for Social Contact

Now, as much as I love individual exercise, there are also some very real benefits to the social contact that group exercise classes provide. Personally, I know that when I was feeling low, demotivated, and isolated, attending my weekly exercise class made a big difference to how I was feeling.

Yoga/Pilates: These are more relaxed, stretching and core focused classes, which make them a great option for all ability levels. They also tend to have an emphasis on mindfulness, which as we will discuss in the next chapter has some great benefits from a mental health and recovery standpoint.

Spin: If you are looking for an intense cardio session in an incredibly motivating group environment this is the class for you. Expect to come out of the class sweaty! There is not as much talking as in other group classes, but there is definitely a great group atmosphere as you all work hard at the same time.

Boxing/Boxercise: There is an output very cathartic about hitting a pad or box as hard as you can for an hour! I tried it myself a few times and I do not think there are many better ways of releasing some frustration. Plus, it is a great cardio workout, and because of the partner-based nature of the class, you will get to know someone else well.

Water-Based Exercise Classes: This is quite a broad category of classes, ranging from general exercise in the water, through exercise to music and even including exercises like synchronised swimming and performance classes. If you love being in the water and want a good chance to socialise, then this is the option for you.

How Many Times Should You Exercise Each Week?

There is no specific number of times that you 'should' exercise per week, and there is no need to put pressure on yourself to complete a certain number of sessions just because someone else is doing so and says that you should   too.

Instead, just do the number of sessions that you want to do. If that is one session, great, if that is three sessions, great.

What I have found works best is just trying to pick several sessions that I know I will be able to consistently do alongside any other commitments.

What to Do When You Do Not Feel Like Exercising?

As I mentioned at the start of this chapter, exercise can often feel like the furthest possible thing from what you want to be doing. In fact, what you will most want to do sometimes in a day might just be to sit on the sofa, wrap yourself up in a blanket and watch bad tv all day. And to be honest I do not think that there is anything wrong with that - up to a point!

Rest, relaxation and time spent doing nothing is completely acceptable, but if it starts to become ALL you are doing then it could be a bit of a problem.

Getting outdoors, seeing friends and looking after your physical health and wellbeing are all important parts of a balanced, happy life, and if you are not doing them, you are really not helping your own recovery.

So, what do you do on those days where you know that you should be exercising, but you just do not feel like it?

Well, you do what I like to call *'momentum building'*.

Let us say that going outside for a run sounds like WAY too much effort.

⇓

No problem.

⇓

Could you do something simple, like put your workout clothes on?

⇓

Great, then start with that.

by Chelsea Berrie

⇓

And after that, okay, well maybe a run still sounds like too
much effort, but how about a short walk around the block
just five or ten minutes, could you do that?

⇓

Okay, so now you are walking, your heart rate is
elevated, you are enjoying the fresh air, could you maybe
walk a little bit further? Something like 20 minutes? And
how about walking a bit faster with nice quick steps?
Perfect.

⇓

Last five minutes now and you are on your way back
home. Those endorphins are kicking in and you are
feeling good. How about a quick run back home instead
of a walk? It takes only a few minutes, should be easy!

You get the idea, right? Instead of seeing exercise as
this all or nothing activity, we are seeing it more as a
spectrum, and starting with the easiest possible version
in order to build momentum.

Honestly, you'd be amazed how many times I did not
want to exercise at all, only to use this method and find
myself getting back in from a really enjoyable exercise
session 30 minutes later.
Seriously, give it a try and you might just surprise yourself
too.

Shinrin Yoku - The Healing Power of Nature

Shakespeare once wrote that "*one touch of nature makes the whole world kin.*" and I think what he was talking about is the unique ability of nature to bring people together. People of every age, race and background can find both relaxation and awe in the great outdoors. In fact, just to make my point, have you ever noticed how on a sunny day, people will almost always choose to sit on the grass instead of man-made substances like concrete or metal (even when they are crafted into nice looking seats and benches)

But what is it about nature that appeals to us on an almost instinctual level?

Well, in Japan, there is a concept known as 'Shinrin Yoku,' which essentially translates into English as 'forest bathing.' The idea is simply that by going out into nature, spending time among trees and greenery, that you will receive health benefits.

I know that might sound a little spiritual and woo-woo, which may or may not be your type, but there is also a good base of scientific literature to back up those claims too. Bratman et al (2015) found that as little as a 50-minute nature walk improved complex working memory and reduced anxiety in participants. Chawla (2015) assessed the existing body of evidence on the effect of nature on children, concluding that nature does indeed have a positive impact on wellbeing, physical and mental health, and even relationships. Shanahan et al (2016) found that nature and wellbeing had a positive correlation; the more

by Chelsea Berrie

time participants spent in nature the lower the occurrence of both depression and high blood pressure. These three studies are just the tip of the iceberg, there are dozens upon dozens of high-quality studies showing that nature really does have a huge array of benefits on both your physical and mental health.

So, what we have got is a completely free way to reduce anxiety, lower blood pressure, combat depression and improve your fitness at the same time. From a recovery perspective, that is what I call a win-win. Plus, since you can see those benefits with as little as 50 minutes time in nature per week, it is very achievable.

If you are interested in learning more about Shinrin Yoku here is a resource you can explore.

Action Steps

Once again, we are finishing this chapter with a set of actionable steps that you can put in place to help you towards your road to recovery, and just as before, do not feel like you have to follow all the steps if you do not want to, these are simply streamlined suggestions to bring together everything we have talked about in the chapter.

1) Pick a type of exercise that you feel will suit you

2) Purchase or acquire any equipment you need, as well as any memberships.

3) Practically, try to schedule exercise sessions into your week, and remember that you will not always feel like training. In those instances, use the 'momentum' approach.

Chapter 5: Mindfulness and Meditation

When I first heard about some friends of mine practising mindfulness and meditation back in the early 2000's, I thought that they had gotten themselves into some form of hippie cult that involved a lot of flowers, sun dresses and chanting. Not that there is view necessarily wrong with that mind you, it was just the first conception my mind associated with those words. Jump forward twenty years and I have downloaded a new mindfulness app on my phone and have 5-minute meditation sessions every single day.

So what changed?

Well, two big differences really...

First, I kept seeing seemingly thousands of people talking about how great it is online. Not just strangers either, but people that I knew personally as well. And second, curiosity got the better of me, so I did a bit of googling, watched a few videos on YouTube and gave it a try.

Honestly, I can say that it is one of the best actions that I have taken for my mental health, not just in recovering from loss (although it was definitely a big help there too) but in so many aspects of my day-to-day life.

In this chapter we will be looking at what mindfulness and meditation are, what their main benefits are, as well as providing some practical examples and recommendations

by Chelsea Berrie

for how to implement them into your own person
recovery process.

Why I have Placed This as Chapter Five in the Book

So, the reason that I have placed this section a little late
in the book is because I wanted you to have a base of les
direct healthy coping mechanisms already in place
Subjects like…

- A support team of friends, family, and therapists
- Arts-based self-therapy options
- Regular exercise and time outdoors

And the reason I wanted these in place is because they
provide the time and the space for you to indirectly work
on your grief. They are all ways that allow you to cope,
look after yourself and improve your emotional
processing without having to directly deal with your grief.

Mindfulness and meditation is a little different, because
you will often find yourself directly exploring your grief,
learning how to examine it, face it and embrace your
emotional response to it. This can be a powerful part of
your recovery process, but it can also be quite difficult at
first, so having other coping mechanisms in place can be
incredibly helpful.

What Are Mindfulness and Meditation?

I was confused at first with these two words, especially since so many people just seem to use the words interchangeably. From my research, though, here is what I have found...

- Mindfulness, simply stated, is the state of being present or aware, specifically, a focus upon the present moment.

- Meditation is "*a practice where an individual uses a technique – such as focusing the mind on a particular object, thought, or activity – to train attention and awareness, and achieve a mentally clear and emotionally calm and stable state*" (Walsh and Shapiro, 2006).

It is quite clear that you can think of mindfulness as a state, and meditation as a practice.

Is Meditation the Only Way to Create Mindfulness?

Not at all. While meditation is proven to help create mindfulness (Carmody and Baer 2008) it is just one of many ways that a state of mindfulness can be achieved.

Other examples include…

- Dialectical Behaviour Therapy (DBT) a form of therapy that emphasises mindfulness the development of mindfulness through building specific skills and having specific conversations.

by Chelsea Berrie

- Mindful eating and drinking, in which you deliberately eat slowly, taking the time to savou each bite and focus on the sensory experience o eating food. Wine tasting is a perfect example.

- Mindful walking, in which you slow down and focu on the feel of the ground, the breeze on your face the smells in the area. Instead of walking just t get from A to B you are enjoying the walk for it own value.

And these are just a few simple examples, realistically yo can turn almost any activity into a mindfulness practice b focusing upon it and engaging in the present momer without distractions. The trick is to slow down, focus o the experience and try to suspend judgement. It is no good or bad, it just is.

Benefits of Mindfulness and Meditation

Alright, so we have established what mindfulness and meditation are, as well as some simple ways to create mindfulness in your day to life, but what are the benefits o doing so?

1) Mindfulness improves self-acceptance and self-esteem.

Research (Thompson & Waltz, 2007) has found that mindfulness practices, and higher ratings of daily mindfulness, are positively associated with better self-esteem and more self-acceptance. I think that by taking the time to genuinely appreciate your everyday experiences, and to understand your reactions to them, you are building a strong understanding of who you are and what you like.

2) Mindfulness and Meditation Reduce Stress

There is no denying that taking some time for yourself every now and again is a great way to reduce stress. No work stress, no emails, no family responsibilities, just a few moments for you to be with you.

They are also great for stress reduction because they can help you to get out of patterns of overthinking about the past, or the future, and be present in the current moment. I know that even before I had experienced any loss, I was always worried about the uncertainty in the future, bills, work, events and other worrying items. Mindfulness helped me to better focus on the here and now, and personally this really helped me to feel less stressed in my day-to-day life.

I am not alone in this experience either, a meta-analysis (Hoffman et al. 2010) examined 39 different scientific studies to conclude that mindfulness and mindfulness-based therapy were positively associated with reductions in multiple measures of stress and anxiety.

3) Can Be Useful When Preparing for and Experiencing Emotional Triggers

One of the challenges to deal with when you are recovering from loss is having to cope with events like

anniversaries, birthdays, and special dates that you know
are strong emotional triggers. You can feel like you are
coping well and doing great on your recovery journey,
only to hit a huge wave of memories and complex
emotions that you must process.

Mindfulness and meditation can be fantastic tools for
these moments, because they give the ability to observe
your thoughts and emotions non-judgmentally. Instead o
beating yourself up or feeling silly for struggling, you can
acknowledge how you feel and know that it will pass.

Moreover, mindfulness and meditation can also be used
to stay relaxed and help you plan for upcoming triggers.
By being aware upfront that your emotional state may
change, you can reduce some of the shock and surprise
when it does.

4) Helps to Combat Depression

I know depression is a topic that people would not like to
talk about, but it affects a lot of us, especially those of us
who have had to deal with the loss of someone close to
us. For me at least, I think that any non-harmful method
that can help to alleviate that depression is a good method.
Mindfulness and meditation have been shown to do
exactly this.

Research (Farb et al. 2010) examined self-reported
measures of depression, stress, and anxiety, as well as
brain responses of two groups of people watching sad
films. One group had engaged in a mindfulness-based 8-
week intervention, while the other group had not. The
researchers found that the group that had done the

mindfulness intervention reported less stress, depression, and anxiety, and had less severe brain responses.

5) Improved Focus

One of the biggest troubles that I had immediately after my loss was difficulty focusing. It was part of the reason I got into problems at work. I would start one task only to find myself doing another without really being clear on when I had switched. Or I would catch myself staring off into space, look at my clock and realised that I had been doing so for about half an hour. Or even better still, when I did try to knuckle down and focus, it was like a hundred different thoughts would all try to rush into my brain at the same   time.

This is where mindfulness-based meditation comes into its own, because it actively develops and improves your ability to calm your mind and focus on the task at hand. Studies (Moore and Malinowski, 2009) have found that people who practice mindfulness-based meditation are less distractible, able to pay closer attention, and are even more mentally flexible when the need arises, for example when a situation or environment changes at the last minute.

6) Makes for Better Relationships

I should admit that I was not the best friend or family member when I was recovering from loss. I was stressed, depressed, anxious, angry, apathetic, and pretty much every other word you can think of that screams *"not much fun to be around!"* And while all those emotions are completely valid responses to loss and grief, I did not want them to have a long-term negative impact on my relationships with people that I cared about.

For me, it was mindfulness and meditation that played a big role in managing to maintain those relationships, and even today, years after my loss, I am confident that my relationships have all benefited from my mindfulness practices. Mindfulness has allowed me to…

- Be less reactive to stressful relationship situations.
- Remain calm and listen to other people properly.
- Better express me and communicate more clearly.

And it is no surprise to me that research (Barnes et al. 2007; Wachs & Cordova, 2007) has found mindfulness scores to accurately predict relationship satisfaction.

Types of Meditation Practice

Meditation practices are incredibly diverse, which is great for us because it gives us a wide range of options to choose from to suit our own personality and preferences. Here are some of the most common forms of meditation practice.

Body Scan (Progressive Relaxation)

This is one of my all-time favourite types of meditation because of how simple and easy it is. It is a great way for beginners to get started.

What you will do is sit or lie down, and then work from head to toe (or vice versa), slowly squeeze and then relax each muscle.

It is that simple.

But the magic is that it draws your attention into the present moment by giving you a specific task and experience to focus on.

Breathing Meditation

This type of mediation is another great option for beginners. Just like with body scan meditation it draws your attention to the present moment by giving you a specific task and experience to focus on your breathing.

You will perform the meditation by breathing slowly and deeply, focusing your thoughts only on your breaths. You may choose to count your breaths, or to follow a certain tempo.

Kundalini Yoga

This type of yoga is essentially a yoga-meditation hybrid that combines slow yoga movements and flows with deep breathing and mantras.

It is a great option if you tend to be someone who struggles to sit or lie still and prefer to be 'doing' something. The slow yoga aspect gives you something to 'do,' but nothing so challenging or engaging as to be distracting from the act of simply 'being.'

by Chelsea Berrie

Mindfulness Meditation

As we have already discussed, this terminology is a bit c
a misnomer, as all types of meditation lead to some
degree of mindfulness.

In this context, what it means is meditation that focuses
on being aware of your present moment surroundings,
including sights, sounds and smells.

Zen Meditation

Derived from Zen Buddhist teachings, zen meditation is
essentially a formalised version of mindfulness meditatio
that also incorporates elements of breathing meditation.

Typically, you will need a quiet room or space where you
will be undisturbed. Ideally you will be facing a wall so as
not to be distracted by any external movements or
stimulus. From there, you will adopt a specific position
such as the lotus or half-lotus and place a lot of focus on
achieving a specific posture.

The idea is to remain focused on your posture and
breathing, allowing thoughts to come and go without
becoming attached to any of them.

For me, this type of meditation seems like it would take a
bit of getting used to, so might be better as something to
move into once you have tried some of the simpler, less
formalised options.

If you are interested, you can find more information here.

Transcendental Meditation

This type of mediation is also spiritual, and the aim is to 'rise above' or 'transcend' your current state of being, hence the name.

The practice itself involves slow breathing alongside concentration on and repetition of a mantra, which is usually prescribed by the teacher. There are some newer, more modern versions of transcendental meditation that allow the person meditating to select their own mantra.

Visualisation Meditation

Visualisation is a well-established concept that is actually frequently used within sports performance. A golfer visualises their swing before they take it, a basketball player visualises their shot before they shoot it. You get the idea.

The idea is to vividly think about a specific object, item, or idea. Perhaps the most famous example is trying to count sheep when you want to fall asleep. You are visualising the sheep to focus your brain, preventing it from getting caught up in dozens of other thoughts.

Most research suggests that visualising is most effective when imagined in first person (looking through your own eyes) and given the richest detail possible. So, if you are imagining the sheep…

- What do they look like?
- How does the sky look?

by Chelsea Berrie

- Are you in a field? What does the field look and smell like?
- If you stroke the sheep, how does its woolly coat feel?

And so on.

The more vividly you can visualise the situation the better it is at focusing your mind.

Practical Ways to Bring Mindfulness and Meditation into Your Own life

Okay, so we have looked at what mindfulness and meditation are, the benefits they can give us, and some different types of meditation. In this section we are going to be looking at some simple, practical ways that you can bring them into your own life.

1) Link Meditation to an Already Established Habit

In my experience meditation is one of those tasks that gets put right at the bottom of your to-do list. Weirdly because it is a task that you can do any time you end up never actually making a specific time to do it.

I recommend linking your meditation time to an already established habit or action. For me, I now meditate for five to ten minutes every night before bed, because I have linked meditation with the habit of getting in bed. When I am winding down for the evening, locking up the house and cleaning my teeth, I am reminding myself that it is meditation time. This stops me forgetting to do it, and the meditation before bed really helps to put my mind at ease to help me sleep.

You could aim to do it in the same way, or you could link meditation practice to another habit of your choice, such as waking up or eating your lunch.

2) Turn Everyday Activities into Mindfulness Activities

You really do not have to go out of your way to make mindfulness practice a part of your daily life. Basic daily activities can be turned into mindfulness activities with the right approach. All you need to do is slow down, focus on the present moment and draw your attention to your senses. Here are some examples…

Mindful Eating: It is easy to get into the habit of wolfing down your food at incredible speeds, not really taking the time to savour it. To eat mindfully you are going to do the opposite. Slow down your eating process and take the time to be present in the moment. How does the food smell? What texture does it have? Is it warm or cold? How does it taste? Not only will you end up enjoying your food WAY more, but you will also be getting all the benefits of mindfulness as part of your daily routine.

Mindful Driving: If you are someone who must regularly drive to and from work, or just as part of your day-to-day life, it can often become an activity that you do on autopilot. Personally, I have even found myself arriving at my destination with no real conscious memory of the journey. Upon reading about this, I found that it is a little memory shortcut your brain does. Essentially, if it thinks there is no new useful information (because you have travelled that trip hundreds of times) it does not try to store it. Pretty much the opposite of mindfulness!

But we can easily turn this into an opportunity fc mindfulness practice by making ourselves mor consciously aware of the trip. What can we see? Hov does the road feel? Does the area have any specifi smells? And if we get stuck in traffic or encounter a ba driver, that is an opportunity to see our thoughts of ange or frustration and let them pass, without holding onto them

Mindful Gardening: Even without the benefits c mindfulness, gardening is a great way to spend some tim outdoors being physically active and connecting with th natural world. With that said, between mowing lawns watering plants and cutting hedges there are times that can feel a little like a chore. To turn it into a more mindfu experience, aim to slow down and really appreciate wha you are doing. How does the garden look, how does sound? Are there birds or bees that you can hear? Hov do the plants and flowers smell?

Mindful Dishwashing: Okay, so this one does not quite work if you load everything into an electric dishwasher. But if you are washing some dishes by hand, this can be a great opportunity to practice your mindfulness and be present in the moment. Rather than letting your mind wander and think about loads of different things, try drawing your attention to how the water feels and how warm it is on your hands. Is the washing liquid scented? Lavender? When you put the dishes in the drying rack, can you place them softly and carefully?

Mindful Exercise: I absolutely LOVE this one, because it is so easy to do. Exercise already takes your focus out of your head and into your body, so all you are really doing is enhancing that. For me, resistance training is where it really works. As I warm up, I like to really feel each muscle and joint start to move and activate. I like to think about my breathing, as well as things like properly bracing my core and abs before lifting weights. I like to think about how the weight feels in my hand, the temperature and texture of the metal. When the lift is finished, I like to pay attention to my heart rate and notice how it is elevated, and when I am cooling down afterwards, I like to focus on my stretches, the individual sensation of each muscle being lengthened.

3) Start Slow - A Little Goes a Long Way

Just like we talked about in the chapter on exercise, it is usually best to start a new skill or activity slowly, and at a pace that you can consistently manage. Starting mindfulness and meditation for the first time by saying that you are going to meditate for one hour every day is probably just setting yourself up to fail. Whereas starting with something like 5-minutes, 5 days per week is very achievable.

You could also try starting by saying that you are going to pick one or two everyday activities from the list above to be more mindful about. Then over time you can add to this list.

In my experience, a little really does go a long way, and if you have been doing nothing before, doing anything at all, no matter how little, is going to be beneficial.

4) Have No Expectations

One of the challenges for most people to get their heads around with mindfulness and meditation is that there is n specific end goal, timeframe, or completion. As a society we are very much geared towards the tangible, as in "if I do X, for Y number of days, I will achieve Z outcome." So, it can be hard to engage with a practice that does no strictly follow that same pattern or logic.

You must go into mindfulness and meditation without expectations. You are performing the practice simply to 'be' rather than to 'do.' There is no end goal. There is no trophy, award, or sticker. You cannot go in thinking that by meditating exactly 17 times you will feel 51% less stressed or anxious, because it is not an exact, numerica process.

To be clear, this does not mean that mindfulness and meditation are not effective, as we have already established that they most certainly are. If you stick with them for long enough it is likely that you will be less stressed, less anxious, less depressed, more self-aware, and more focused. All I am saying is that you should not put pressure on yourself for all those meditating actions to happen, because they are a by-product of the process rather than the end goal.

5) Try a Guided Meditation

The last practical tip I have got for you is to try a guided meditation. If you are feeling a little indecisive and you cannot seem to pick from the options I have provided, then it can be great to simply switch on a guided meditation and follow along. This is also a great option if you have been trying self-driven mindfulness or meditation but have been struggling with it.

If you go to YouTube and type in mindfulness meditation you will find plenty of good videos, or if you go to a music service like Spotify or apple player you will find various audio tracks that you can use.

Another option is to download a mindfulness app on your phone or tablet, for example Headspace, a handy little app with the tagline *"be kind to your mind"* that has specific guided audio sequences of meditation, mindfulness, stress relief and sleep, as well as guided meditations focused on certain topics like relaxation, empathy and gratitude.

Seeing the Loved One You Lost During Meditation

I can pretty much guarantee that at some points during your meditation your thoughts are going to turn towards the person you have lost. In fact, it is probably going to happen a lot.

That is completely okay.

It is normal, it is natural, and it certainly does not mean that you are bad at meditating. It is exactly one of the reasons meditations are so useful when dealing with your loss. You can use this as an opportunity to practice acknowledgement without over-attachment, to let the image and memory of your loved one come into your mind, watch it, observe it, and then allow it to leave without getting caught up or fixated.

To be honest, sometimes you might struggle. The thought and the image might stick or be hard to observe without a large emotional response. But over time, and with practice, it will get easier.

Plus, it is important to remember that if it gets too much, you can always end the meditation and use any other of your other healthy coping mechanisms such as calling a friend, family member or therapist, exercising or doing some creative, arts-based activity.

Frequently Asked Questions on Mindfulness and Meditation

I think it would be best to round this chapter off with some of the most frequently asked questions about mindfulness and meditation, so you have got simple and accessible answers right from the start.

Do I need to meditate for a certain amount of time per week?

Not at all, there are no set or strict guidelines for time you spend each week. Realistically the amount of time that you meditate or work on your mindfulness is completely up to you. Some weeks you might do more, others you might do less. Either way, there are still plenty of benefits to be had.

Is there a best type of meditation?

There is no 'best' type of meditation or mindfulness practice, and honestly, I have no idea how anyone would even go about measuring that. At the end of the day, it is all about finding what works for you.

What does it mean if I have a bad session?

If you have a 'bad' session, as in a meditation or mindfulness session in which you struggled to let thoughts go, struggled to relax or struggled to focus, it means one thing…

You are human.

Everyone has better and worse days, but by making the effort to meditate and be mindful (even if you struggled) you are taking a step in the right direction and you will be that little bit better at dealing with the situation next time.

How do I know when I am not being mindful?

A lack of mindfulness comes across in three ways…

1) Constantly distracting yourself rather than being engaged in the present moment, for example playing on your phone while watching TV, or worse yet, playing on your phone during family mealtime.

2) Going through your day on autopilot, not taking the time to appreciate anything or anyone around you.

3) Acting in ways that are not congruent or in-line with

who you consider yourself to be and the values that you hold.

Is Mindfulness and Meditation Good for All Ages?

Absolutely, the ability to calm your mind, be present in the moment and manage your emotions is a fantastic skill for all ages. There is increasing amounts of research suggesting that implementing small, simple elements of mindfulness into primary schools can have positive effects on learning and behaviour.

Do I need to wear any specific clothing?

I get asked this question a surprising amount when I talk to people about mindfulness and meditation. Do not worry there is no special gown or robe you need to wear (unless you want to, that is!) Just wear whatever you are comfortable in. Personally, I find that nice, loose clothes are best, and I tend to avoid tight fitting jeans or tops that might interfere with my breathing.

How long will it take for me to become mindful?

There is no set time frame to become mindful, and mindfulness is not an object that you have or do not have, rather it is more like a spectrum or sliding scale in which you can be mindful.

Are there any useful mindfulness books I can buy?

Personally I really enjoyed a book by Jon Kabatt-Zinn (2007) called Coming to Our Senses: Healing Ourselves and the World Through Mindfulness.

I cannot sit still for more than 5 minutes - what gives?

Mindfulness and meditation are a skill, and it takes a bit of practice.
Today we are encouraged to be constantly go-go-go. Buy this, do that, play this, see that. Combine that with so many new technologies assisted models of instant gratification and you have got a set-up in which sitting, relaxing and not doing anything feels incredibly weird. Heck, I used to sit for all of 2 minutes before I was itching for something to do.

But have you ever noticed how a cat is quite content just to sit and watch the world go by? Or how a bird can rest on a perch for hours not really doing anything?

And have you noticed how UN-stressed they are?

Just saying.

Be more cat. Be more bird.

Seriously, though, start with small sessions and aim to build up over time. Your ability to sit, focus and be mindful of the present moment will improve, just stick with it.

by Chelsea Berrie

Action Steps

Let us wrap up this chapter with a set of actionable steps that you can put in place to help you towards your road to recovery. Do not feel like you must follow all the steps if you do not want to, these are simply streamlined suggestions to bring together everything we have talked about in the chapter.

1) Pick one or two everyday activities that can easily be turned into mindfulness practice.

2) Decide on a type of meditation that you feel will suit you.

3) Practically, start slow, with no expectations, and keep your sessions short. You can increase frequency and duration as your focus and emotional control improves over time.

*****Please Leave a Review for my work so far*****
As an independent author with a small marketing budget, reviews are my livelihood on this platform. If you enjoy this book so far, I would really appreciate it if you could leave your honest positive feedback. Thank you!
You can do so by clicking the link below. I love hearing from you, my readers and I personally read every single review.

*****link to review page*****

&&&&__You are welcome to join our group to learn some tips you may never heard of to enhance your mental performance__&&&

Chapter 6: Music and Recovery

I am sure you have seen plenty of films where someone is sad or depressed, or dealing with the loss of someone close to them, and all they seem to do is have their headphones in, living in their own little world of emotional music. It is a real trope, and once you start looking out for it you will see it everywhere!

Fun fact though, for the first two or three months after my loss, I did not listen to ANY music. For me, at least, it just felt too emotionally triggering. Sometimes I would hear a lyric that reminded of the person I had lost, and others it would just be the emotional impact of the instruments themselves that would set me off. Practically speaking, it wasn't exactly ideal trying to go and do my weekly shopping, only to have all my makeup smudge because I'd been crying when a cold play came on the radio.

So if someone had told me then that music could actually be a useful tool in my recovery process, I'd have probably given them some serious side-eye!

You can imagine my surprise, then, when I stumbled upon an article by Douglas MacGregor talking about how music is "*one of the most powerful tools we have in the face of loss*" and that it was a huge part of how he dealt with grief over the death of his mother.

With that in mind, I felt that I owed it to myself to do a little investigating, and in this chapter, I want to share with you the results of my search. We will be looking at how and

by Chelsea Berrie

why music and grief are so connected (with a little culture and history lesson) as well as the major benefits that music can bring during the grieving process. In the end of the chapter, we will be looking at some ways to implement music practically and sensitively into your recovery journey, so that you can see it is beneficial without becoming too emotionally triggering like it was for me at the start.

How and Why Are Music and Grief So Connected?

Music has incredibly strong ties to rituals and ceremonies throughout history and across numerous different cultures. Births, coming of age ceremonies and funerals were all traditionally linked to specific songs, dances, and music. For example

- The Yolngu of Northern Australia use very performance driven musical funeral rites to mourn and celebrate the deceased. The songs and music last for about two weeks and are believed to help the bereaved move from raw emotion though to a social, collective contemplation and remembrance of their loss.

- Then there are Gaelic songs of lament, dating back at least to the 16th century (Henigan 2015) which express the emotional loss of the bereaved. The process is called 'keening,' and comes from the gaelic term *caoineadh,* meaning 'to cry' or 'to weep.'

- There are also Shi'a Muslims across south Asia, who collectively seek to direct some of their own personal mourning into specific religious chants that lament the death of Husain, son of Mohammed.

And these are just a small handful taken from dozens of examples.

It is only within modern western cultures that songs and music have taken somewhat of a backseat in the grieving process, in place of a far quieter, more solemn experience.

That is not to say that modern western countries do not have music or songs at funerals, rather it is to say that these songs are not often sung by the people attending, and are commonly chosen specifically for the individual, so they do not have the same communal meaning or tradition. While celebrating the individual interest is great, the downside is that the communal aspect is lost, which could be negative when it comes to healing, as the people grieving do not have the same level of community support.

The Benefits of Music for Recovery from Loss

Okay, enough history lesson for one day! Let us talk about the benefits of music when recovering from loss.

Music allows for self-discovery.

One of the big surprises I encountered when I eventually did start listening to music again (about 3 months after my loss) was that it seemed to unlock some emotions that I

had not even really registered. That is one of the rea
benefits of music, that whether through listening or playing
you get to discover more about yourself by tapping int
something beyond verbal expression.

Music allows us to remember.

Music is incredibly evocative, and it can bring bac
cherished memories of the person you have lost, allowing
you to maintain a sense of love and connection. Studie
(O'Callaghan et al. 2013) have found that listening t
familiar music, and finding new music related to the
deceased, go a long way to continuing bonds.

Music connects you to your body.

Listening to music is not just an auditory experience
Music makes you dance, it makes you move, and by
combining the two things you can achieve a hugely
cathartic experience.

Even if you do not have much rhythm, simple things like
running to music can make a huge difference to how you
are feeling, more so than either of the things would have
done on their own.

Music is a great way to relax.

We all need a break sometimes, and music is a great way
to relax. It is for exactly this reason that almost all spas,
as well as almost all meditation and yoga classes involve
some form of music. For me, there is just some feeling
very soothing about listening to soft, gentle music that
really allows me to unwind. Studies (Allen et al. 2001)

have even shown that music can help to reduce stress, anxiety, and blood pressure in patients before, during and after surgery.

Music creates a space for grief.

Just with the arts-based therapies we discussed in chapter 4, one of the main benefits of music is that it can create a space in which complex emotions can be expressed without having to rely on verbal communication. We all know that talking about death and grief can be incredibly difficult, but through music we can connect, share how we are feeling and find support without having to say a word.

Music is transformative.

Again, just as with arts-based coping methods like drawing or painting, writing, creating, and playing music can be a transformative process that allows you to take complex and often troubling emotions and turn them into some experience beautiful. It might sound strange, but to some people knowing that their turmoil and sadness can be transformed into a new positive mindset is incredibly important in their recovery.

Music can improve how you process grief.

There are some interesting studies showing that music can play an important role in improving people's ability to cope with and process grief. The first study (Thomas 2005) looked at adolescents aged 12-18 and found that weekly music therapy led to improved scores across all domains of their grief process scale. The second study

(O'Callaghan 2013) looked at caregivers supporting terminally ill cancer patients and found that music was used to improve mood and confront grief before the loss of the loved one, as well as serving to continue bonds and improve coping after the loss.

Practical Ways to Make Music Part of Your Recovery Process

Okay, so we have looked at some of the benefits that music can bring to your recovery process, but how do we practically work it into your life? And most importantly, how do we do so without becoming overwhelmed by the emotions that music can trigger? In this section we are going to answer those questions.

1) It Does not Have to Be All or Nothing

Just because I went from not listening to music at all for three months to researching most days does not mean you have to. In fact, I would say that is a pretty poor way to go about it.

Your relationship with music does not have to be an all or nothing situation. Instead, you can use your own judgement about how much to include, as well as when and where. If you know that you find music very emotionally triggering, then start slow, and only use it for small amounts of time when you feel up to it.

2) Choose Times and Spaces Without Pressure

Look, the absolute least you want to do is to try to listen to an album of songs that remind of the person you have lost in the middle of your workplace. You might also want to avoid car journeys, because crying as you try to drive simply is not safe.

Instead, try to choose times and spaces in which you will not be under any pressure, and where you will have the chance to experience the emotions, react in your own way, process them, and then recollect yourself. This can be on your own, or with trusted close friends and family, the important part is that it is a space in which you feel safe.

3) Use a Mixture of Songs

You do not have to listen to a solid hour of sad songs just because it seems like the appropriate thing to do while grieving. You can listen to absolutely any music you want and experience any emotions that come along with it.

Personally, I ended up finding that what worked for me was listening to 2 or 3 songs that reminded me of the person I had lost, followed by 2 or 3 more upbeat songs to ease me back into day-to-day life. I found that this gave me a good balance between time to reflect and remember, versus getting caught up in a day long depression funk.

4) Try Combining Music with Movement

by Chelsea Berrie

When I want to relax, one of my favourite things to do is perform some slow, yoga style stretches alongside listening to relaxing, instrumental music. All I can say is that the combination of the two seems to be more powerful than either of them on their own. The music allows me to feel more focused on my movements, while my stretching and movements help me feel more grounded and, in the moment, which helps to stop me from overthinking.

If you have twenty to thirty minutes free in the evening, try this and I can almost guarantee that you will sleep so much better than usual.

5) Listen to What You Want

During my research I ended up finding dozens of websites suggesting specific songs to listen to while grieving. I am sure that they were trying to be helpful, but I really failed to see how listening to multiple songs in styles and genres I do not enjoy, by artists I do not particularly like, was going to help me.

The reality is that musical taste is very individual, and that what 'speaks' to me might not 'speak' to you, and vice versa. So instead of feeling like you must listen to some pre-agreed collection of songs, let your own interest guide you.

6) Practice Mindful Listening

Back in chapter 5 we talked all about the benefits of mindfulness and staying in the present moment. You can combine this practice with your music listening. To do so, direct your focus to the present moment, *what can you hear? Which instruments are playing? If there are vocals, how do they sound?* Moreover, when feelings and thoughts arise, your goal is to observe them non-judgmentally and then let them go, almost like watching clouds overhead. It is a skill that takes practice, but over time it can have a huge selection of benefits.

With all that said, you certainly do not have to practice mindful listening all the time. It is also completely okay to listen to music freely or for fun. You might also want to listen to music while letting your mind wander and thinking about the past or the future. In short, mindful listening is just one possible way to engage with music.

7) Keep a Music Journal

If you agree with me, you will probably find that your emotional responses to music can be all over the place, and often unexpected. Sometimes my responses would be intense, and other times I would be much quieter, calmer and more collected. I found that a useful part of the process for me was keeping a music journal where I would record some of my responses throughout the week.

For me, this gave me a way to think about and clarify what I had experienced and provided me with much needed time to reflect. Plus, it also gave me five to ten minutes to compose myself, calm my emotions and get myself ready to re-enter my day-to-day life, almost like having a cool down after an intense exercise session.

Give it a try for a couple of weeks and see what you think.

by Chelsea Berrie

Action Steps

Let us wrap up this chapter with a set of actionable steps that you can put in place to help you towards your road to recovery. Do not feel like you have to follow all the steps if you do not want to, these are simply streamlined suggestions to bring together everything we have talked about in the chapter.

1) If you have been avoiding music because it is emotionally triggering, make sure you read the section of the benefits of music for long term recovery.

2) Pick a selection of music that speaks to you personally, and do not feel like it all has to be sad songs. You can use a combination of any music that works for you.

3) Practically, choose times and spaces in which you feel safe, and in where you have time afterwards to process your thoughts, ideally in a journal.

Chapter 7: Daily Wisdoms & Contemplations

As you move further through your recovery process and develop better coping mechanisms, you will find that you can think of the person you lost, and the process might not be so emotionally raw.

It is not so obvious without specifying the fact that it is not just the loss of a loved one that we must deal with, it is the loss of a huge part of our world view, beliefs, and identity.

The world can never *"return to normal"* as some people might tell you, because you have forever been changed by experience. You are not the same person anymore.

And a big part of the later stages of your recovery is coming to terms with that and taking the time to re-evaluate who you are, what you believe and what you think about the world around you. Plus, doing all of that without becoming overwhelmed.

To help you with that, I will be using this chapter to look at the benefits of contemplations, as well as provide 12 short quotes, wisdoms, and contemplations for you to think about. Everything from life and love through to death, meaning, soul and purpose.

The Benefits of Contemplation

by Chelsea Berrie

Improved Focus

Contemplation by its very nature is a focused observation of a specific object or idea. By practicing the skill of focusing for an extended period, you should see this carry over into other areas of your life.

If, like me, you struggled with focus after your loss, then this could be a great way to rebuild that ability and get your mind performing how you want it to.

Empathy and Acceptance

By taking the time to think deeply about topics you will be able to gain a lot more understanding of what other people might be thinking or feeling. In our day to day lives it is easy to become very 'me-focused,' especially when we are busy, which can lead to us downplaying, ignoring, or not even considering the needs of others. By taking the time to slow down and think, you are providing yourself with the opportunity to empathize with others and imagine what walking a mile in their shoes with grains of sand inside might be like.

Similarly, research (Bruce 2018) has shown that contemplation increases our tolerance towards others even when they are doing or saying what we may not directly agree with. This is a crucial part of life, because you are never going to agree with every single person, nor are you going to like his/her single comment on the world you live in. But by increasing your ability to tolerate these personalities being not as you want them to be, you increase your ability to live your own, healthy, stress-free then happy life.

From the perspective of a recovery from loss, there is one obvious fact that you do not like, and that is the loss of the person you cared about, the fact that you would obviously change if you could. By improving your ability to accept and to tolerate, you are improving your ability to cope with that loss.

Appreciate Nuance

Bear with me on this because I am going to go on a little rant...

Throughout human history people have been divided into camps of 'them' and 'us,' often spurred on by political or religious leaders. Over time this creates distrust, animosity, and conflict.

In the United States today Democrat Vs Republic is a perfect example...

To certain democrats, all republics are just out of touch, ultra-conservative, racists who do not want to listen to anyone else's opinion.

And to certain republicans, all democrats are just lefty liberal snowflakes that get offended by anything and everything in the world.

Yet that just is not reality. Both 'camps' actually include a diverse mixture of viewpoints and ideas, which vary significantly by age, gender, town, state, ethnicity and economic status. The problem is that this complexity does not make for a very catchy banner or slogan, it is not very marketable, and the complexity gets massively over-simplified.

by Chelsea Berrie

By taking the time to contemplate and to think deeply about topics, you get the change to unravel their complexity and come to a deeper, more nuanced and more accurate understanding.

And I can promise you, it makes for a much healthier, nicer, and happier way to live.

Because life is short, and it doesn't matter who you are or what you believe, we all love, we all want to be loved, we all die, and we all experience loss.

Less Likely to Make Fear-Based Decisions

There is a region of our brain called the posterior cingulate cortex, and it is activated when we think about ourselves, such as our fantasy, our daydreams. Now, while this can be useful for visualising ideas and imagining ourselves in situations, it can also work to our detriment by engaging us vividly to imagine worst case scenarios. This is especially true for those of us who have been through a loss, or through another traumatic event. What this means is that we can end up making decisions based on our brain vividly creating the least realistic, absolute worst possible case scenario for every event. Not a good path to go down.

Luckily, contemplation has been shown to reduce the activation of your posterior cingulate cortex during these 'worst case scenario' imaginations. By contemplating, we are training ourselves to stop, think deeply and take a more rational approach, so we become far more able to stop the 'worst case scenario' train in its tracks.

Reshape Your Worldview

Just as we talked about above, the loss of someone close to you changes you in ways that you might not have expected. It also changes the way you view the world, and the way that you think about different topics. Heck, did you ever notice that you started to talk about topics that had never even crossed your mind before?

Never once in my life had I stopped to think about the *'meaning of life'* or *'what it makes a memory'* or any other topics like that.

Then suddenly my brain sort of tried to process all of those questions all at once!

For me, regular small amounts of deeper contemplation allowed me to reshape my worldview and redefine where I fit within it. I think it will do the same for you too.

The Importance of the Timer

I recommend that you set a 5–10-minute clock timer so that there is an enforced limit to the amount of time that you can ruminate. I have personally found that there is a fine line between useful and detrimental, and it tends to be around the 10-minute mark. In all my sessions that were less than 10 minutes I came away feeling clearly, more at peace and it seemed I knew a little bit more about myself. Whereas in some of my sessions that went on longer than 10 minutes I found myself becoming really bogged down in thought, lowering my mood, and having an unproductive day.

by Chelsea Berrie

Think of these contemplations almost like medicine. When taken in a small, regular, and prescribed dosage they can be incredibly useful in your healing process. But when taken too often or in too high a dose, the side effects can be potentially harmful.

An Important Reminder

You do not have to do these every day, if you are feeling quite low and do not feel up to it, then you can take a day off.

Plus, at this point in your recovery process you should have a good sense of which healthy coping mechanisms work for you. If you find a contemplation session too difficult or emotional, then you can call one of your support team (friends, family, therapist) or use creative arts, music or exercise to calm your mind.

Daily Contemplation Number 1

"You are not 'in the now;' you are the now. That is your essential identity-the only thing that never changes. Life is always now. Now is consciousness. And consciousness is who you are. That's the equation."

Eckhart Tolle

Prompts

- What does living in the moment mean to you?

- How can you more fully experience the present moment?

Daily Contemplation Number 2

"Death will indeed come, whether or not we are prepared."

Atisha Dipamkara Shrijnana.

Prompts

- Can we prepare for death?

- Knowing that death is coming, would you do anything differently?

Daily Contemplation Number 3

"Learn to be quiet enough to hear the genuine within yourself so that you can hear it in others."

Marian Wright Edelman

Prompts

- What are your core values?

- How can you better listen to others?

by Chelsea Berrie

Daily Contemplation Number 4

"Life is too deep for words, so do not try to describe it, just live it."

C. S. Lewis

Prompts

- What can you do today that you would enjoy?

- Are there any words that you could use to describe life?

Daily Contemplation Number 5

"Enjoy the little things, for one day you may look back and realize they were the big things."

Robert Breault

Prompts

- What is the event that you are taking for granted right now?

- Can you think of three events to be grateful for?

Daily Contemplation Number 6

"The most beautiful people we have known are those who have known defeat, known suffering, known struggle, known loss, and have found their way out of the depths. These persons have an appreciation, a sensitivity, and an understanding of life that fills them with compassion, gentleness, and a deep loving concern. Beautiful people do not just happen."

Elisabeth Kubler-Ross

Prompts

- When you read the above quote, did anyone come to mind in particular?

- How can you be more compassionate to others?

Daily Contemplation Number 7

"Life is not a matter of milestones, but of moments."

Rose Kennedy

Prompts

- What are three of your favourite moments?

by Chelsea Berrie

- What can you do today to create a new moment?

Daily Contemplation Number 8

"I have learned that people will forget what you said, people will forget what you did, but people will never forget how you made them feel."

Maya Angelou

Prompts

- How did the person you lost make you feel?

- How can you make others feel happier?

Daily Contemplation Number 9

"There is a sacredness in tears. They are not the mark of weakness, but of power. They speak more eloquently than ten thousand tongues. They are the messengers of overwhelming grief, of deep contrition, and of unspeakable love.

Washington Irving

Prompts

- How do you express your emotion?

- When was the last time you cried?

Daily Contemplation Number 10

"Death ends a life, not a relationship."

Jack Lemmon

Prompts

- How can you honour the memory of the person you lost?

- How do new relationships balance alongside this?

Daily Contemplation Number 11

"I do not believe people are looking for the meaning of life as much as they are looking for the experience of being alive."

Joseph Campbell

Prompts

- What does being alive mean to you?

- Do you ever feel like you are looking for a meaning to life?

Daily Contemplation Number 12

"The meaning of life is just to be alive. It is so plain and so obvious and so simple. And yet, everybody rushes around in a great panic as if it were necessary to achieve something beyond themselves."

Alan Watts

Prompts

- What do you think the meaning of life is?

- How can you more fully experience day to day life?

Action Steps

This chapter has been incredibly action-oriented already, so these are simply some of the key points...

1) Pick a time and space in which you feel safe to

process complex emotions and thoughts/

2) Set a timer to limit how much time you spend in this headspace.

3) Work through a single contemplation in a session.

by Chelsea Berrie

Chapter 8: Learning to Celebrate and Honour the Person You Lost

I need to emphasize there is a reason why this chapter is one of the last in the book. It is here because quite simply, it is often not a topic you are ready for in the immediate aftermath of your loss.

In fact, if someone had told me in the first few weeks after my loss to focus on celebrating the person I had lost, my response would have been...unpleasant.

In the first few days, weeks, and months after your loss, I can all feel so raw and so emotionally charged, that the idea of moving towards a quiet acceptance and a form of celebration can seem impossible. You are dealing with shock, sadness, anger, loneliness, numbness, and a whole other bunch of emotions that simply come into play with priority.

If you are in the early stages of loss, and you have jumped to this chapter without reading chapters 1 through 7, then I really recommend going back and taking some time with those, because you will probably find them much more useful for where you are at. Plus, speaking from experience here, your focus needs to be on building support systems and finding healthy coping mechanisms.

Who Is This Chapter For?

Realistically, this chapter is for if you have read chapters 1 through 7 and spent a decent amount of time putting some of the recommendations I made in place. That includes...

- You will have a support system of friends, family, and therapist.

- You will be actively engaging with creative arts or music as a method of emotional expression and healthy coping.

- You will be getting outdoors, engaging with the world around you and ideally taking part in some type of regular exercise each week.

- You will also be doing some deep inner work based around either mindfulness, meditation, journaling and/or daily wisdom and contemplations.

Because by following the above-mentioned helpful steps, over time you will find yourself able to think more positively about the future. And your feelings of the loved one you have lost will be manageable. You will be able to think of, acknowledge the thoughts and emotions that come with them, and then let them go, as if observing clouds in the sky. In short, you can cope, and you are progressing fantastically on the road to recovery.

What is This Chapter for Then?

You might be wondering, *"If I am already progressing on*

my road to recovery so well, then why do I even need this chapter?" Good question.

The truth is that recovery from loss is not just about accepting that you have lost someone and lessening your emotional response over time. Of course, that's part of it, but it is not the whole story.

The whole story is more about reframing and re-evaluating the way that you think about the person you lost. It is the difference between…

being able to think about the person you lost without crying.

and

being able to think about the person you lost and smile.

And that is a HUGE difference.

Because over time, you will want to honour the person that you lost, and you will want to be able to look back on your memories with them and remember the good times you had together. Remember the person they were, the values they represented, the lessons they taught you.

And that is only truly possible when you learn how to celebrate them.

So that is exactly what we are going to do in this chapter.

How to Transition into Celebration

I think it is important to start by noting that just because you are moving into a place where you can celebrate and honour the person you lost, does not mean that you no longer get to feel sad, or miss them, or cry. All those feelings are still completely natural, and healthy, be human and allow the recovery a reasonable timeframe.

Now, with that clarified, I want to share with you three activities that I have personally used to help me transition from a place of grief to a place of celebration.

1) '10 Things I Hate About You'.

Have you ever seen the movie 10 things I hate about you? It has Julia Stiles and Heath Ledger as the two romantic leads, and it is essentially a cheesy, feel-good 90's retelling of Shakespeare's The Taming of the shrew.

There is a scene in the film in which Kat (Stiles) reads a poem in front of the class, on the 10 things she hates most about Patrick (Ledger)...

by Chelsea Berrie

I hate the way you talk to me,
and the way you cut your hair.
I hate the way you drive my car,
I hate it when you stare.
I hate your big dumb combat boots,
and the way you read my mind.
I hate you so much it makes me sick,
it even makes me rhyme.
I hate the way you're always right.
I hate it when you lie.
I hate it when you make me laugh,
even worse when you make me cry.
I hate it when you're not around,
and the fact that you didn't call.
But mostly I hate the way I don't hate you,
not even close,
not even a little bit,
not even at all.

Now, maybe I am just a big old sappy romantic comedy fan, but there is something quite special about this type of poem. It basically takes lots of little details about a person that should be incredibly annoying or frustrating and shows just how inconsequential they are in the face of love.

And you might think I sound a little crazy here, but <u>I want you to do the same thing.</u>

It does not have to rhyme, in fact it does not even have to be a poem if you do not want. Bullet points can work just as well. But it needs to be 10 things that wind you up about the person you have lost.

But how does this help me deal with loss?

Simple, it gets you remembering the person you have lost for who they truly were, faults and all. When we lose someone there is this tendency to remember only the good about them, to paint them in an unrealistic light that is not reflective of the person. Instead of pretending that the person you lost was perfect, you get to acknowledge their faults, address their pet peeves, and conclude that you loved them anyway, despite their imperfections.

The process also makes you laugh. In creating your list, you will have to think back on so many different humorous events and situations. That time they did not put their wet towel back on the radiator for the hundredth time! The way they used to mispronounce that word, over and over again! This ability to look back and laugh is a huge part of your recovery process.

2) Share Stories with Others Who Knew Your Loved One

Another activity that I found incredibly helpful in my recovery process was taking the time to connect with other people who knew the person I had lost. Sometimes they knew them closely, other times they only knew briefly or in some small way, but each and every time I felt like it was a positive experience.

Sometimes we'd share a story or experience that we had in common, which was great for laughs and nostalgia.

Other times someone would tell me about something I thought I knew, only from a different angle, which gave me a clearer picture.

And sometimes I'd learn something completely new and random that I had no idea about, which opened up whole new undiscovered things about the person I'd lost. (dance club in college!)

For me, not only did sharing these stories allow me to remember, and even learn, about the person I had lost, they also got me considering how that loss had affected other people all around the world. Both from my experience, and from the others that I know, it is quite common for your focus and attention to move inwards after a major loss. It is completely natural, because you are suddenly having to process a lot of information and emotions. Over time, though, reconnecting with the wider world, socialising, and empathising are all crucial parts of your recovery process.

To get started then, I want you to draw up a quick list of people who knew the person you lost and contact some of them asking if they want to meet up for a coffee, a chat or have a conversation by phone if they are further distant.

You might also want to consider using the internet, for example creating a page or social media post where people can share their memories.

3) Gratitude

It can be hard to find what to be grateful for, especially after a loss. And people telling you to be grateful often just makes you feel frustrated and resentful, because you would probably give up all the things you are supposed to be grateful for just to have some more time with the person you lost.

However, gratitude, when used CORRECTLY, can be a powerful tool in your recovery process.

For me, I like to start by thinking of, or journaling, the experience that I am grateful for about the person I lost. What did they bring to my life during our time together? What am I grateful that they created for me or provided me with?

And the benefit about doing this is that they come easily.

From there, with my mind primed to think a little more positively, I like to move onto more general gratitude. What am I grateful for today? In my life right now? In the world around me?

Gratitude does not have to be a kind of emotion complex. You could be grateful for a friend or family member's support. Grateful for the food you ate. Grateful for the roof over your head. Grateful for your favourite TV show. The point is that there is always something to be grateful for, and by turning your attention towards those things you are moving yourself towards a much healthier mental space.

So, the three activities you have are…

- '10 things I Hate About You'
- Sharing Stories
- And Gratitude

by Chelsea Berrie

Nothing particularly complex or confusing, just three simple strategies that when put together can help you transition towards a place of celebration.]

You will acknowledge the whole person, for good and bad.

You will share stories, learn more about them and gain new perspectives.

And you will focus on what you are grateful for about your time together.

Ways to Celebrate and Remember

Okay then, if you have worked through some of the activities above, you are hopefully in a headspace in which you want to celebrate and remember the person you lost. In this section we are going to be looking at some specific examples of ways that you can do that, broken down into four main categories; a place to remember, an object to remember, an activity to remember, and a legacy to remember.

A place to remember.

It can be helpful to have a physical space in which to remember and celebrate your loved one. Across the world, shrines are used for exactly this reason, often complete with flowers, candles, and religious icons. Practically, a version of this that you could use is to have a corner of a room filled with pictures, photos and items that remind you of the person you lost.

Another option is to have a specific location or place that you visit. For a lot of people this is simply the grave of the person, but you could also use locations that have a specific memory or meaning for you and the person you lost.

Personally, I know a couple of people who have commemorated their loved ones by sponsoring a bench to be built in a spot that they liked, or for a plaque to be added to an existing bench. Oftentimes you will be able to speak to the local council and they will be happy to help.

An object to remember.

Sometimes, having a physical reminder of the person can be a way to celebrate them. Some examples of this are wearing a piece of jewellery that they gave you, or one that has a picture of them inside.   It is also becoming increasingly popular to keep a small amount of their ash locked inside a piece of jewellery. Or, if you happen to have a few thousand dollars to spare, there is the option to take your loved one's ashes and use them to create a brand-new diamond.

It does not mean that your object must be jewellery though, and there are plenty of other great examples of objects that can be used to remember and celebrate the person you lost…

I know some people who have taken an item of clothing like a jacket or coat and taken to wearing it every so often.

by Chelsea Berrie

I also know others who have especially kept objects lik
old cameras and books that were favourites of the perso
they lost.

There is no right or wrong way to remember and celebrate
it is all about finding something that feels special an
meaningful to you.

An activity to remember.

We build memories through activities, through the things
that we do with the people around, and so it is also
through activities that we can honour and remember
them.

For example, if they were a keen cook, and some of your
best memories of them were based around the kitchen,
then how about cooking up their favourite meal?

If they enjoyed playing the guitar, and you remember the
house being filled with music, how about playing it
yourself occasionally?

Or if they loved sports, and you would play games
together, then why not play a game occasionally now?

You get the idea.

By engaging in the activities that formed your bonds, you
are honouring what made your relationship with that
person unique, and you are remembering a key part of
who they were and what was important to them.

A legacy to remember.

Perhaps what we all fear most is to leave this earth without leaving a mark or a legacy. That is why we apply ourselves to tasks and ideas, to careers and projects. We hope to leave some legacy behind. You can honour this and celebrate the person you lost by working to continue their legacy and build upon the projects or planned work they cared about.

For me, this meant engaging more with nature, gardening, planting trees, spending time outdoors, and aiming to reduce my environmental impact. I did not really care too much about the above-mentioned work when I had still my loved ones alive with me, since the work meant a lot to my loved ones, and so I made a promise to myself that I would honour my loved ones by continuing what was important to them.

For you, this might mean something completely different…

If your loved one cared about youth opportunities, then perhaps you could volunteer some time to support local youth groups and projects?

If your loved one believed that sport was an option for improving someone's life, then you could consider starting a small scholarship fund alongside local high schools and colleges.

Or if your loved one used to bring charity change to the homeless, then why not think about working with a local homeless shelter a few times per year?

by Chelsea Berrie

Birthdays, Anniversaries and Religious Holidays

Now, I know first-hand that birthdays, anniversaries, an
religious holidays can be difficult times of the year after yo
have experienced a loss. You will often find yourse
feeling heightened emotions and your mind will often dri
towards thoughts of the person you have lost. To help yo
deal with this, it can be a good idea to put some health
remembrance and celebration activities around thes
times.

- Visit their grave.
- Hold a memorial/remembrance party.
- Look through old photos and videos.

Plus, you should feel free to include any of the ideas an
suggestions in the previous section. Organizing an
taking part in activities that remind you of the person yo
lost or doing something that honours their legacy.

Over time, you will find that although the feelings of los
never truly go away, you will be able see these occasion
as opportunities to celebrate the person's life, and to buil
new positive memories for your future.

No 'Right Way'

Hopefully you are getting the sense by now that there is
no right or wrong way to remember and celebrate the
person you lost, which I know might sound obvious, but is
actually really important to hear.

When I was looking for ways to celebrate, remember and honour the person I'd lost, some of their family had different ideas, to the point where they actually made me feel quite bad about the ways that I'd chosen to honour my loved one. The truth is that they were not even especially close to the person, and I knew that because I had only ever had brief encounters with them in the ten years prior.

The reality is that your relationship with the person you lost is unique, and nobody else can fully understand what they meant to you. You have had your own ways of communicating, your own shared activities, your own jokes, and games. This means that the only person who can decide how best to celebrate and honour their relationship with you, is you.

It is also important to remember that honour, celebration, and memory are unlimited resources. Just because one person has chosen to honour someone one way does not mean that someone else cannot honour them another. If you want to plant a tree it does not stop anyone else from donating to a charity. Keep that in mind.

Fingers crossed, of course, that there are no disagreements, I just wanted to make sure that you knew there could be. Everyone responds to loss differently, but unfortunately not everyone will think to read books like this, and not everyone will have the emotional intelligence to realise that they are acting unreasonably in grief.

by Chelsea Berrie

Action Steps

As with previous chapters, we are going to be finishing with a set of actionable steps that you can put in place to help you towards your road to recovery. You do not have to follow all the steps if you do not want to, these are simply streamlined suggestions to bring together everything we have talked about in the chapter, and help you honour and celebrate in your own way.

1) Work through at least 1, or ideally all 3, of the 'transition into celebration' activities.

2) Decide on your own personal place, object, activity and legacy to remember your loved one.

3) Practically, if possible, think of ways to plan for milestones and anniversaries that may be triggering, using them as opportunities to create new, positive memories.

Chapter 9: Hopes, Dreams and Looking to the Future

And here we have arrived at the final chapter of the book, one which deals with what I would consider to be the last stage of your recovery process, looking to the future.

I want to emphasise before we start that this is written as the last chapter in the book for a reason, and that I want you to have read through the previous chapters of the book before you go through this final chapter. I cannot expect everyone to take all the methods described in our book in the precise order, especially when it comes to dealing with loss, although it is still recommended that you follow the essential steps to help your recovery.

However, there are certain measurements that you need to have in place to really engage with and see the benefits of this chapter.

If you remember back to chapter 1, we talked about moving towards a helpful view of grief, and we imagined ourselves lost at sea among a storm. Right after your loss it feels like you are drowning, and more than anything you are just struggling to cope. In that situation it makes absolutely no sense whatsoever to be thinking about and planning out your future. Your energy, both mental and physical, needs to be directed towards surviving. It is only after you have built yourself a raft, rowed back to shore and had time to recollect yourself that you can truly begin to start thinking about the future.

by Chelsea Berrie

Make sense?

Who Is This Chapter For?

Just as with chapter 8, this chapter is for you if you have...

- Built a support system of friends, family, and therapist.

- Been actively engaging with creative arts or music as a method of emotional expression and healthy coping.

- Been getting outdoors, engaging with the world around you and ideally taking part in some type of regular exercise each week.

- Been regularly doing some deep inner work based around either mindfulness, meditation, journaling and/or daily wisdoms and contemplations.

Additional, though, I would ask that you have worked through chapter 8 and taken some suggestions so that you have

- An honest, whole person view of the person you lost. A view that you can think on and smile with.

- A place, object, activity, and legacy through which to remember and honour the person you loved.

To continue our lost at sea metaphor. You are already back home. The traumatic event is no longer fresh in your memory and you have had the time to rest, reflect and re-evaluate. I cannot tell how long this will take, as the amount of time varies for everyone. But you should be in a mental space in which you are ready to look towards the future with hope.

Why Do You Need Hopes and Dreams for the Future?

In a book with an entire chapter on mindfulness and the benefits of staying in the present moment, it might seem slightly counterintuitive to conclude with a chapter all about hopes and dreams for the future.

And yet, if we do not talk about them, I feel we will be missing out on a quintessential part of the human experience, because to hope and to dream is human. It is part of what gives us life, part of what makes us who we are. And even if all we want is to stay peacefully focused on the present moment, we must still have hope in our hearts for that to be the case.

Put simply, to hope and to dream is part of life. Having persons and things to love and to look forward to is what makes life worth living. And it is the ability to embrace all these in life and move forwards that is fundamental to our recovery from loss.

Remembrance Vs the Future - A Story of Guilt

Guilt is a horrible emotion. Especially guilt that you sort of know you should not be feeling, and yet are feeling anyway. It is a weird kind of self-aware guilt that makes no sense.

For me, I knew, logically that I had to move forward with my life. I had to meet new people, go to new places and have new experiences. And yet every step I took towards the new life somehow also felt like a step away from the person I had lost. It was not rational, it was not sensible, and I even knew that the person I'd lost would absolutely be laughing at me for worrying about it. But none of that stopped me genuinely feeling guilty for moving on with my life.

Turns out, it is not just me either, or that this guilt is a kind of emotion that a lot of people experience when dealing with a loss. Moreover, in cases where the loved one was lost in a tragic accident or traumatic event, people often experience a severe guilt known diagnostically as *'survivors' guilt.'* The idea that you could have or should have done something differently or noticed some signs beforehand, when as a matter of fact, there was no way that you could have had.

The truth is that guilt is not always a logical or rational emotion. It is a complex emotion. For me, this meant that I felt like I had to visit my loved ones grave a certain number of times per year, as well as remembering them in specific ways and specific times. And while there is nothing wrong with remembering and honouring the person you have lost; you should never have to feel guilty because you planted your loved one's favourite plant's seeds a day later than planned so that you could see your friends on Saturday. (Yep!)

How did I move past this?

Well, it took me so long before I recognized it as an unhealthy pattern, and I mentioned it to my therapist, who worked with me to explore the reasons for my guilt and help me to find ways to move past. In a word, just being able to talk to someone about my feelings went a long way to solving the problem.

Importantly, I also think that I had to give myself permission to move on. It is almost as if I was waiting for something, a sort of magical sign to tell me that it was okay, or a signed letter directly from the Pope, Buddha, or Gandhi. I was the only one who could give myself permission to move on and live my own life. Once I accepted this, it was almost like a weight had been lifted.

The same goes for forgiveness too. Sometimes the guilt we feel is because of all the words we think we should have said, or the tasks we should have done, or could have done differently. You must stop and recognize that you already did what you could do based on who you were and what you knew at the time. You must forgive yourself. And if there are lessons to be learnt, then use them to enrich your future relationships and actions, rather than using them as reasons to hold yourself back.

You and Them - Finding What YOU Want

When I went through this process myself, thinking about hopes, dreams, and the future, I found myself in a weird situation of self-doubt that I hadn't seen coming. Turns out, living for others is easier than it is to live for yourself.

by Chelsea Berrie

It might sound odd, but hear me out.

Everyone had been telling me, I am sure with the best of intentions, that moving on and living my life was exactly what my loved one would have wanted me to do. To be happy, to be healthy and to live my life to the fullest. And as you have seen in the previous section it took me some time, but eventually I completely agreed with them.

The problem was that before big decisions I would oftentimes ask myself the question…" *what would they [my loved one] have wanted for me?"*

- Would they want me to continue in my stable career or put myself at financial risk to pursue my dreams?

- Would they want me to live on my own and keep my independence, or move back in with family or friends for extra support?

There was no way to know, and all it did was get me bogged down, stopping me from making any kind of decision.

The reality was that I had not quite yet worked out who I was and what I wanted WITHOUT the person I had lost. (I guess I should have spent more time with the daily contemplations from chapter 7) and so I had to set about rediscovering me.
And my guess is that you might have to do the same thing.

Let us start with the question...

What do YOU want for you?

What are your goals? What are your dreams? How do you want to live? Who do you want to meet?

And believe me, I get it, they are not easy questions. So perhaps I should share some ways that worked for me…

Try <u>starting with what you do not want,</u> and work from the opposite of there…

- Do not want to work an office job - okay, keep it going.
- Do not want to be lonely - okay, onto the next…
- Do not want to live in the city - alright.

And so on and so forth.

In the example above, we know that the person wants to live outside the city, near to a group of close friends or family, and work in a job that has them either outside or in a dynamic, physical type of environment. That is a good start.

So, right now, I want you to start by taking ten to fifteen minutes to write down the top ten that you do not want in your life. Then, I want you to take the opposites of the top ten and flesh them out with a bit of detail.
Continuing the example above, the person wanted to live outside the city, so to flesh this out they could think about whether the suburbs, or a much smaller town or village is what they are looking for.

The process of adding to a fleshing out your wants may take a while, that's completely normal, just remember that

by Chelsea Berrie

it is an important part of your recovery process, and a big step towards living a life that brings you joy.

Grief and Growth - Myths and Misconceptions

You might have noticed a trend, or rather a recurring trope among books and articles about loss.

That grief is somehow automatically associated with growth.

I am talking about the imagery of butterflies and rainbows, the inspirational stories of people who changed their entire lives after a loss, built a multi-million dollar business with only two dollars and donated it all to charity, all while achieving the body of their dreams, mentoring vulnerable youths and adopting sixteen puppies.

Of course, I SOMEWHAT exaggerate, but you know exactly the kind of story I am talking about, and while it might seem harmless on the surface, I think it put a lot of pressure on people recovering from loss to somehow undergo some kind of miraculous personal transformation.

In this section I want to break down three of the biggest myths and misconceptions surrounding grief and growth.

Myth Number 1: You will Become a Better Person After Grief

Okay, so this one absolutely winds me up, and here is why. You *might* become a better person. But you might also become a miserable one. Sorry for the language, but it is totally a possibility. Whom you will become is not set yet in cement. There is no guarantee that a traumatic and life-changing event is going to magically make you a better person.

The reality is that yes, you will change after a loss, but how you change is complex and multi-faceted. If you are someone who follows the advice in this book, works with a therapist, builds healthy coping habits, and does plenty of deep inner work to build emotional intelligence, then there is a good chance you will be moving in the right direction. On the other hand, if you are someone who does not do any of that, you could be looking at a quite different outcome.

Myth Number 2: You NEED to Grow or Change After Grief

In fact, when I experienced my loss, I was senseless with my life. For me, I did not especially want to *'grow'*, whatever that meant, I wanted my loved one back and I wanted to go back to how the life was.

Now, as I write this, I realise that I have changed, and probably grown in some areas, quite a lot. But that was never my goal or my plan I set out to achieve. To be honest, I just wanted to feel 'normal' again, and be able to cope with day-to-day life.

If you are drowning in the ocean, all you want to do is get to dry land. You really do not care if you are a better, stronger, or more emotionally mature person when you get there!

Myth Number 3: Growth and Change Has A Set Endpoint

See, this is the problem with the butterfly metaphor. It is caterpillar, it is in a cocoon and then BAM, it is a beautifu butterfly. Top marks, job done, huge transformation visibl completed.

The truth about humans is that WE ARE NO CATERPILLARS, we are constantly changing an adapting, sometimes for the worse, sometimes for th better.

- The changes are not always huge, in fac sometimes they are barely noticeable.

- And they are never complete. We never reach point in our lives in which we go, *"yep, this is i perfection is achieved."*

And when we put this expectation on ourselves, or whe others put it on us, we tend to devalue the work that w have done, because it is somehow not enough or does no count.

My Message to You

As humans, we have this 'fantastic' ability to beat ourselves up for absolutely no reason. We put pressure on ourselves to do certain tasks and accomplish certain goals in specific timeframes. And if we deviate from the plans and targets by even the smallest amount, we start labelling ourselves 'failures' or 'lazy' or 'broken.'

Seriously, I want you to try and stop that nonsense, especially when you are dealing with a loss.

It is completely okay to focus on living each day as best you can, looking after yourself, and being present in the moment.

You do not have to become someone else, and you do not have to undergo some huge, miraculous personal growth.

Looking towards the future should be fun, not a chore. There is no need to bury yourself under the weight of insane expectations.

Stop being so hard on yourself.

Looking Towards the Future - 3 Ways to Plan and Make Goals Without Putting Too Much Pressure on Yourself

Okay, so if you did not read the section above, go back and read it now. In fact, even if you just read, go, and read it again. What I said there sets the tone for everything we are going to discuss in this section here. We want to find ways to look towards the future and make plans without putting pressure on ourselves, and to help you with that I

by Chelsea Berrie

am going to share three methods that I have personally found helpful.

1) Start by Recognizing the Difference Between High-Achievement and Perfectionism

If you are like someone who naturally gravitates towards setting themself goals and working hard, then you have probably also had to deal with the battle against perfectionism. You see, high achievement is exactly what it sounds like, aiming high, and setting out to achieve a lot. Perfectionism on the other hand is setting your aim so high, that it becomes impossible to reach the goal that you set. For example,

"I am going to write a book and aim for 80% positive reviews."

Vs.

"I am going to write a book and aim for 100% positive reviews".

The first sentence is high achievement, writing a book is a tough job to do, and achieving majority positive reviews implies hard work, good research and quality writing.

The second sentence is perfectionism, because you are saying that even if you achieve an overwhelmingly positive 99% good reviews, you have still failed to accomplish your goal, which can lead you to feel bad even though you have actually achieved an amazing goal.

Make sense?

Looking towards the future after loss works in the same way. It is completely okay to set yourself goals, and if you want to set high goals then that is fine too. What you need to avoid, however, is setting yourself goals so high that you cannot achieve them. In the real world there is not such a thing as perfect, and it can really help to remember that.

"I am going to be a good, attentive parent to my children".

It is a great goal, whereas…

"I am going to be the best, most attentive parent in the world".

It is perfectionism.

"I am going to go out a few times to meet new people".

Is an extremely healthy, positive goal, whereas…

"I am going to make 10 new friends and find 3 potential life partners".

Is perfectionism.

2) Focus on Process-Oriented Goals Rather Than Outcome-Oriented Goals

If you have never heard these terms before, process-oriented goals are goals that focus on the steps and actions required to achieve specific goals over time. Outcomes goals on the other hand are goals to specify the achievement for a certain rule. To use a simple example, let us talk about weight loss…

"I am going to exercise three times per week and eat more vegetables".

It is a process-oriented goal.

Whereas…

"I am going to lose 2 stone".

It is an outcome-oriented goal.

I should mention that outcome goals do hold some purpose, they help to give a specific goal post to aim for or accomplishment to achieve, so if you are naturally driven by achievement, trophies, or rewards then these types of goals can be motivating. The problem is that these types of goals also place a tonne of pressure on you, especially when it feels like you might not accomplish them. They also do not account for factors outside your control which might impact the outcome. For example,

Let us say that a saleswoman is hired in a car showroom and told that she needs to make 10 sales per month. (An outcome goal) She does great for a few months, but then a news report starts circulating about issues with the car. She is still expected to make 10 sales per month, but customer interest has been reduced, and so now she is under loads of pressure to achieve an outcome outside of her direct control.

On the other hand, let us say that the same saleswoman was given process-oriented goals, such as 'spend X number of hours trying to contact potential customers,' or 'spend Y hours per day on the sales floor.' she would be under far less pressure, and management would be able to accurately monitor her performance despite fluctuations in market demand.

So how do we apply this to setting goals after loss?

Simple, we focus on the process rather than the outcome...

"I am going to meditate 3 times per week" rather than *"I am going to become more mindful"*

"I am going to paint twice per week" rather than *"I am going to become more emotionally expressive"*.

I promise, not only will you put far less pressure on yourself, but you will also end up being more likely to accomplish the desired outcome, because you have given yourself actionable steps to follow.

3) Double Check Your Emotional State Before, During and After Making Plans

I think we can all be prone to making emotionally driven decisions from time to time, I know I certainly am. Unfortunately, when recovering from a loss, our emotions

do not always tend to be the most stable or consistent, s
how we feel one day can vary quite a lot from how we
feel the next.

In my case, I'd have some days where I felt really good,
at peace, and ready to move forwards, so I'd make a
bunch of plans that required a lot of commitment.

And then a few days later I'd be feeling rough, missing
the person I'd lost, and not feel like doing anything befor
the bare essentials.

So I'd essentially alternate between making really
ambitious plans and then not wanting to make any plans
for the future at all.

Over time, what I found useful was to start double
checking my emotional state before, during and after
making plans. I would ask myself questions like…

- How am I feeling?

- Am I feeling scared? stressed? Or pressured?
  (Because trust me, fear-based decisions never
  seem to end well)

- Do I feel the same about these plans now as I did
  before? And if I feel differently, why might that
  be? Does it correlate with my emotional state?

And by asking these questions I became better a
identifying which plans to commit to, and which ones t
move to the side-lines. I also gained a better overall grasp

of how my emotional state could impact my decision making, which really helped me learn to trust my judgement.

To put this into action for yourself, I recommend starting by using a journal so that you have a physical, written record of your thoughts, emotions, and decisions. Then, after a few weeks, you will find that you are able to look back through your journal and start noticing trends, patterns, and common occurrences.

Yes, it takes a bit of work, but I can promise you that the benefits are worth it.

Action Steps

And that is the end of our final chapter. Just as before, let us wrap up with a set of actionable steps that you can put in place to help you towards your recovery. You do not have to follow all the steps if you do not want to, or if you are not ready for them yet. They are simply streamlined suggestions to bring together everything we have talked about in the chapter.

1) Give yourself permission to move forwards, stop feeling guilty, and if relevant, forgive yourself.

2) Be aware of and challenge the 3 big myths about grief and growth.

3) Start setting yourself pressure-free goals and plans based on my 3 recommendations (avoid perfectionism, focus on the process, double check your emotional state)

Conclusion

And we reach the end of our time together. We have covered…

Grief (Re)Education. Including the major myths surrounding loss and a healthier 'ocean' metapho framework for recovery.

Building Your Support Team. Exploring the benefits anc common misconceptions surrounding therapy, as well as how to educate your friends and family so that you car empower them to support you in the ways you deserve.

Creative Coping. Specifically, how painting, writing poetry, and other creative arts can offer invaluable anc unexpected pathways to recovery.

Exercise to Heal. Where we looked at the benefits of exercise while recovering from loss, as well as practical suggestions and guidance for implementing exercise intc your life effectively and sustainably.

Mindfulness and Meditation. Including key benefits like combating stress and reducing the impact of emotional triggers, plus specific ways to bring meditation and mindfulness practices into your day-to-day life.

Music and Recovery. How some technique that I avoided for so long can play a key role in relaxation, self-discovery and grief processing.

Daily Wisdoms and Contemplations. Where we looked at various quotes of life, love, death and meaning to facilitate manageable doses of deep inner work.

Learning to Celebrate, Honour and Remember. Specifically, how certain activities and tasks can help move you towards celebrating your loved one, and the numerous ways in which you choose to honour them.

Hopes, Dreams and Future Plans. In which we talked about giving yourself permission to overcome guilt and move forwards, the myths surrounding grief and growth, and three useful pieces of advice for making plans without putting too much pressure on yourself.

And I have got to admit, it has been quite an emotional book to write, but I really do hope that you have found it useful in your road to recovery, and that my own experiences and research can make your journey just that little bit easier.

Before we go, though, I want to leave you with a final thought.

Recovery from loss is not easy. In fact, it is probably the hardest thing that anyone can do. It is a process that you did not want, you did not ask for, and yet you still must play an active role in. With all that in mind, it is so important that you *show yourself some compassion.*

It is okay that it is hard. It is okay to struggle. It is okay to have days where you feel like you are doing well, just like it is okay to have days where you feel terrible.

by Chelsea Berrie

At the end of the day, though, try to remember that you do not have to be alone through this. There are other people out there who can, and will, help you. They might be friends, they might be family, they might be therapists, they might be a local support group, or they might even be an online forum or discussion group.

There is absolutely no shame in asking for help, or in telling people that you are struggling. In fact, I would not even argue that asking for help is an incredibly brave action to take.

That is it from me, so I will leave you with one of my favourite lines…

"Time is too slow for those who wait, too swift for those who fear, too long for those who grieve, too short for those who rejoice, but for those who love, time is eternity."

Henry Van Dyke

*****Great You Reach the end of the book-Please Leave a Review for my work*****
As an independent author with a small marketing budget, reviews are my livelihood on this platform. If you enjoy this book, I would really appreciate it if you could leave your honest positive feedback. Thank you!
You can do so by clicking the link below. I love hearing from you, my readers and I personally read every single review.

*****link to review page*****

&&&__You are welcome to join our group to learn some tips you may never heard of to enhance your mental performance!__&&&

by Chelsea Berrie

References / Further Reading

Achor, S. (2010). The Happiness Advantage. New York City, New York: Penguin Random House

Allen, K., Golden, L. H., Izzo, J. L., Jr, Ching, M. I., Forrest, A., Niles, C. R., Niswander, P. R., & Barlow, J. C (2001). Normalization of hypertensive responses during ambulatory surgical stress by perioperative music. *Psychosomatic medicine*, 63(3), 487–492.

Alpert, Jonathan. (2012). In Therapy Forever? Enough Already. The New York Times. Retrieved from http://www.nytimes.com/2012/04/22/opinion/sunday/in-therapy-forever-enough-already.html?_r=0

Barnes, S., Brown, K.W., Krusemark, E., Campbell, W.K. and Rogge, R.D. (2007), The role of mindfulness in romantic relationship satisfaction and responses to relationship stress. *Journal of Marital and Family Therapy*, 33: 482-500.

Beauregard M. (2014). Functional neuroimaging studies of the effects of psychotherapy. Dialogues in clinical neuroscience, 16(1), 75–81.

Bratman, G., Daily, G., Levy, B., Gross, J. (2015) *The benefits of nature experience: Improved affect and cognition.* Landscape and Urban Planning. Volume 138, Pages 41-50.

Bruce, M. A., Skrine Jeffers, K., King Robinson, J., & Norris, K. C. (2018). Contemplative Practices: A Strategy to Improve Health and Reduce Disparities. International journal of environmental research and public health, 15(10), 2253.

Buchheim A, Viviani R, Kessler H, Kächele H, Cierpka M, et al. (2012) Changes in Prefrontal-Limbic Function in Major Depression after 15 Months of Long-Term Psychotherapy. PLOS ONE 7(3): e33745

Carmody, J., & Baer, R. (2008). Relationships between mindfulness practice and levels of mindfulness, medical and psychological symptoms, and well-being in a mindfulness-based stress reduction program. *Journal of Behavioral Medicine*, 31, 23–33.

Chawla, L. (2015) Benefits of Nature Contact for Children. *Journal of Planning Literature*. Volume: 30 issue: 4, page(s): 433-452

Farb, N. A., Anderson, A. K., Mayberg, H., Bean, J., McKeon, D., & Segal, Z. V. (2010). Minding one's emotions: mindfulness training alters the neural expression of sadness. *Emotion* (Washington, D.C.), 10(1), 25–33.

Goldman, L. (2014) Life and Loss: A Guide to Help Grieving Children. 3rd edition. *Routledge.*

Haeyen, S., Susan van Hooren, Giel Hutschemaekers, Perceived effects of art therapy in the treatment of personality disorders, cluster B/C: A qualitative study,

The Arts in Psychotherapy, Volume 45, September 2015, Pages 1-10.

Henigan, Julie (2015). Literacy and Orality in Eighteenth-Century Irish Song. UK: Routledge. p. 85.

Hofmann, S. G., Sawyer, A. T., Witt, A. A., & Oh, D. (2010). The effect of mindfulness-based therapy on anxiety and depression: A meta-analytic review. Journal of consulting and clinical psychology, 78(2), 169–183.

Moore, A., & Malinowski, P. (2009). Meditation, mindfulness and cognitive flexibility. Consciousness and cognition, 18(1), 176–186.

National Sleep Foundation (2021)
https://www.sleepfoundation.org/press-release/national-sleep-foundation-poll-finds-exercise-key-good-sleep

O'Callaghan et al. (2013) Sound Continuing Bonds with the Deceased: The Relevance of Music, Including Preloss Music Therapy, for Eight Bereaved Caregivers, *Death Studies*, 37:2, pg. 101-125,

O'Connor M. F. (2019). Grief: A Brief History of Research on How Body, Mind, and Brain Adapt. *Psychosomatic medicine, 81*(8), 731–738.

Yann Quidé, Anke B. Witteveen, Wissam El-Hage, Dick J. Veltman, Miranda Olff (2012)
Differences between effects of psychological versus pharmacological treatments on functional and morphological brain alterations in anxiety disorders and major depressive disorder: A systematic review,

Neuroscience & Biobehavioral Reviews, Volume 36, Issue 1, Pages 626-644,

Shanahan, D. et al. (2016) Health Benefits from Nature Experiences Depend on Dose. *Scientific Reports*. volume 6.

Stine L. Nielsen, Lars B. Fich, Kirsten K. Roessler & Michael F. Mullins (2017) How do patients actually experience and use art in hospitals? The significance of interaction: a user-oriented experimental case study, *International Journal of Qualitative Studies on Health* and Well-being, 12:1

Stuckey HL, Nobel J. (2010) The connection between art, healing, and public health: a review of current literature. *Am J Public Health*;100(2):254-63.

Thomas, D. & Krout, R. (2005). Development of the Grief Process Scale through music therapy songwriting with bereaved adolescents. *The Arts in Psychotherapy*. 32. p.131-143.

Thompson, B. L., & Waltz, J. (2007). Everyday mindfulness and mindfulness meditation: Overlapping constructs or not? *Personality and Individual Differences*, 43(7), p. 1875–1885.

Wachs, K., & Cordova, J. V. (2007). Mindful relating: Exploring mindfulness and emotion repertoires in intimate relationships. *Journal of Marital and Family Therapy*, 33(4), p. 464–481

Walsh, R., & Shapiro, S. L. (2006). The meeting of meditative disciplines and western psychology: A mutually enriching dialogue. *American Psychologist*, 61(3), p. 227–239.